little and friday.

CELEBRATIONS

Kim Evans

Photography by Tamara West

PENGUIN BOOKS

PENGUIN BOOKS
Published by the Penguin Group
Penguin Group (NZ), 67 Apollo Drive, Rosedale,
Auckland 0632, New Zealand (a division of Pearson New Zealand Ltd)
Penguin Group (USA) Inc., 375 Hudson Street,
New York, New York 10014, USA
Penguin Group (Canada), 90 Eglinton Avenue East, Suite 700, Toronto,
Ontario, M4P 2Y3, Canada (a division of Pearson Penguin Canada Inc.)
Penguin Books Ltd, 80 Strand, London, WC2R 0RL, England
Penguin Ireland, 25 St Stephen's Green,
Dublin 2, Ireland (a division of Penguin Books Ltd)
Penguin Group (Australia), 707 Collins Street, Melbourne,
Victoria 3008, Australia (a division of Pearson Australia Group Pty Ltd)
Penguin Books India Pvt Ltd, 11, Community Centre,
Panchsheel Park, New Delhi – 110 017, India
Penguin Books (South Africa) (Pty) Ltd, Block D, Rosebank Office Park,
181 Jan Smuts Avenue, Parktown North, Gauteng 2193, South Africa

Penguin Books Ltd, Registered Offices: 80 Strand, London, WC2R 0RL, England

First published by Penguin Group (NZ), 2013
10 9 8 7 6 5 4 3 2 1

Copyright © Kim Evans, 2013
Copyright © Photography Tamara West, 2013

The right of Kim Evans to be identified as the author of this work in terms of
section 96 of the Copyright Act 1994 is hereby asserted.

Designed and typeset by Anna Egan-Reid
Prepress by Image Centre Ltd
Printed in China by Leo Paper Products

ISBN 978-0-143-56901-5

A catalogue record for this book is available
from the National Library of New Zealand.

www.penguin.co.nz

CONTENTS

During the year this book was being created I reflected a lot on what was most important in my relationships with family and friends, remembering all the good times, the laughter and coming together to enjoy each other's company. Christmases, birthdays and weddings all stood out among my cherished memories, but also less formal events, such as each summer travelling on the ferry to Waiheke Island for a family picnic – always a big day full of fun and laughter.

for the large group, but everyone brought their specialty – such as Aunty Marg's Christmas Cake and Mum's pav – so the load was shared.

As a child, I remember being consumed with excitement on Christmas Day, when all the cousins, aunts, uncles and grandparents came together to eat and relax. It was a big effort to prepare food

Nowadays we can feel too busy to make the effort, and with family members often living overseas it becomes harder to bring everyone together, but I hope you will find inspiration in these pages to create many gatherings to share with your family and friends.

Bear in mind that not all celebrations need to be grand. A picnic can simply be to celebrate your relationship with your partner, at a beautiful sun-filled location (like ours at Mt Victoria) with no phones, no kids, just the two of you and some really

paper and chalk especially versatile for setting the theme for a lot of the parties, and for the wedding we hung strips of white crêpe paper and white roses to soften the walls of the local Sea Scouts' hall.

Recipes were chosen so that the majority can be prepared days in advance, reducing stress on the day of the party. Some recipes are more complicated, such as the wedding cake featured on the cover, but there is no reason why anyone cannot produce that and the more complex cakes in this book. I do suggest that you read the Helpful Hints carefully before you get started and also that you give yourself plenty of time to bake and to decorate – don't leave it all to the final hour.

good food. An outdoor Movie Night can be a great way to get to know the people in your street. You supply the food and the sheet for the screen, they bring their own furniture and you all relax and chat over great food and a film. And, if your event includes children, try to create a bit of magic for them, as we did with our Easter hunt.

The most important piece of advice I can give you is to delegate. Don't try to do it all by yourself. A group of good friends is a great resource, providing any gear you don't own, helping to solve any problems and to get through all the tasks quickly and efficiently.

No matter what the occasion, remember it is the simple act of coming together to eat that makes a gathering special and creates good memories to last a lifetime.

Every occasion in this book was created on a limited budget with the focus firmly on delicious food and gathering in a relaxed way – not on formality, fancy venues and fancy gear. For our celebrations we chose spots around Devonport close to my first Little and Friday café, and dressed them up using simple materials. I found brown

HELPFUL HINTS

Essential advice to read before you get started.

Equipment

There is one piece of equipment that I could not live without; it is my trusty electric mixer. I highly recommend investing in a good freestanding electric mixer with a range of attachments: a paddle for creaming butter and sugar, a whisk for whisking eggs and cream and a dough hook for making bread and dough. The recipes in this book are based on an electric mixer, so if you are beating by hand you may need to double the recommended time.

Oven Know-how

The temperatures stated in this book are for fan bake, so if using a conventional oven you may need to increase the oven temperature by about 20°C. Using fan bake helps to move air around the oven, so you can cook several cakes at once. Some ovens have hot spots and you may need to rotate items halfway through baking for a more even result. All ovens are different; older models in particular can vary. Get your thermostat checked if you are finding recommended cooking times consistently inaccurate. I suggest checking baked items 10 minutes before the recommended cooking time.

Tins

I prefer metal baking tins to silicone, as the heat from the metal helps to create a crust on a cake or pastry case.

To grease tins, I use cooking spray but you can melt butter and brush it over the inside of the tin. I recommend using baking paper cut to fit the bottom of the tin and the sides. It is worth the extra preparation time, as you get a cleaner shape to your cake and tins are also easier to clean.

Spring-form tins make removing a cake easier, but they are not essential.

We never grease tins when cooking shortcrust pastry. When baking mini tarts, place a thin strip of baking paper in each tin before lining with pastry. Once cooked, you can simply lift out the cooked pastry cases with the baking paper.

Filling Tins

Once baking soda or powder is added to wet ingredients it starts working immediately. Because of this, you want to get your mixture in the oven as soon as possible. Any tin should not be filled to more than two-thirds full. Make sure to spread the batter evenly so it is flat.

Baking Cakes

Ideally cakes should be placed in the centre of the oven. If you are baking several cakes at the same time, try to give them space so the air can circulate around the oven. If they are on separate shelves, don't place them directly over each other. When checking on your cakes, open and close the oven door gently – do not slam it. It is better not to open the oven at all during the first quarter of the baking period. Cakes can be tested by inserting a wooden skewer in the centre; if the skewer comes out clean, the cake is ready.

Eggs

We use size seven eggs. I highly recommend free-range for baking as they create a much nicer cake. Make sure to bring eggs to room temperature before using.

When you are combining eggs and sugar, make sure to mix them straight away. Do not leave them to sit, as the sugar will burn the egg yolks. Meringues and macaroons work better with older eggs (around 10 days old) than with fresh.

Beating Egg Whites

Bring eggs to room temperature and ensure bowl and beater are clean and dry. There are three stages that the eggs will go through: the first is foam; then soft peaks; and finally stiff peaks. The peaks are found by dipping in your finger and pulling it out – a stiff peak should hold its form. At the soft-peak stage the points will droop over.

Chocolate

For baking we use 50 per cent cocoa solids, nothing less, as it will definitely alter the cake's flavour. Chocolate should be stored at room temperature in a dry, airtight container. Be careful to keep it away from strong flavours such as onions or spices as it will absorb their flavour. To melt chocolate, chop or grate and place in the top of a double boiler or a glass or stainless-steel bowl over a saucepan of simmering water. Do not allow the bottom of the bowl to touch the surface of the water as the chocolate will burn and seize.

Compound chocolate is a substitute product made from cocoa, sweeteners and vegetable fat, which is easier to melt and work with. We use it for chocolate decorations.

Cocoa

I recommend using Dutch cocoa, which is of a superior quality and will give your baking a richer chocolate taste.

Sugar

We use caster sugar in all of our baking because it dissolves more quickly and easily than regular white sugar.

Demerara sugar and muscovado sugar are less refined sugars that contain more molasses and have a stronger flavour.

Glucose Syrup

When making candies, glucose syrup is used in place of sugar to prevent crystallisation. Glucose syrup can be found in most supermarkets.

Flour

Unless otherwise stated, the recipes in this book use plain or standard flour. For breads and doughs, we use high-grade flour. It is higher in protein (gluten), which strengthens the dough.

Unsalted Butter

Bakers only ever use unsalted butter and add salt separately to taste. Like chocolate, butter should be kept in an airtight container away from strong flavours. Make sure to bring it to room temperature and cut it into cubes before using.

Creaming

To ensure maximum incorporation of air into the mixture when creaming butter and sugar, first bring the butter to room temperature and cut into cubes. Using an electric mixer, beat until the texture is smooth and fluffy. There should be no grains of sugar left in the mixture.

Yeast

I prefer to use fresh yeast but it can be difficult to find, so recipes in this book call for instant dry yeast. Instant yeast can be mixed with other dry ingredients without the need to activate it in liquid first; however, it works a little slower and so the dough will take longer to rise. If substituting fresh yeast, double the amount of yeast called for and add it to the liquid ingredients before combining with the dry ingredients. Active dried yeast is different again and needs to be activated by mixing it with the liquid ingredients and a little sugar; stand for 10 minutes before adding to the dry ingredients.

SUMMER PICNIC

You don't need a special occasion to enjoy eating in the fresh air. Pull together an easy outdoor lunch with wholesome picnic food wrapped in tea towels and transported to your favourite leafy spot. Choose dishes that will travel well and which are easy to serve.

Chicken Roulade

Savoury Tarte Tatin

Turkish Pide

Blueberry Poppy Seed Loaf

Chicken Roulade

This recipe has been adapted from Penny Oliver's fabulous
book, *Harvest*. It makes a hearty lunch dish.

1 tbsp extra virgin olive oil

1 onion, diced

2 cloves garlic, crushed

250g pork mince

¼ cup chopped Italian parsley

1 cup breadcrumbs (see
Kitchen Notes)

1 egg

salt and freshly ground pepper

6 slices prosciutto

2 double chicken breasts,
skinless

10 slices bacon

handful of basil leaves

4 hard-boiled eggs

Makes one 25cm roulade

1. Preheat oven to 180°C.
2. Heat olive oil in a frying pan over medium heat and cook
   onion and garlic until translucent.
3. In a bowl, mix pork mince, parsley, breadcrumbs, egg and
   cooked onion mixture until well combined. Season with salt
   and pepper.
4. Lay two sheets of aluminium foil on top of each other on the
   bench. Lay slices of prosciutto crosswise down centre of foil,
   slightly overlapping the slices.
5. Place chicken breasts in a plastic bag and flatten, using
   a rolling pin or mallet. Lay flattened breasts over the
   prosciutto.
6. Spread mince mixture over chicken breasts, then top with
   bacon, slightly overlapping the slices. Top with torn basil
   leaves, then line up hard-boiled eggs down the middle.
7. With the long side facing you, roll up the roulade in the foil,
   forming a tight roll. Twist the ends of the foil to seal. Place on
   a baking tray and cook in centre of oven for 1¼ hours.
8. Remove from oven and allow to cool before unwrapping.
   Store in refrigerator for up to two days.

Kitchen Notes

To make breadcrumbs, place 4 slices bread in an oven preheated to
150°C for 20 minutes. Cool, then crush in a plastic bag using a rolling
pin, or blitz in a food processor.

Savoury Tarte Tatin

This recipe makes two individual tarts. Prepare the tomatoes and Onion Jam a day in advance. Ideally the pastry should be chilled in the refrigerator overnight.

1 sheet Flaky Pastry (see page 182)

4 beefsteak tomatoes, halved

extra virgin olive oil

1 tbsp chopped thyme leaves

1 tbsp chopped oregano leaves

salt and freshly ground pepper

¾ cup Onion Jam (see page 186)

200g goat's cheese, crumbled, plus extra to serve

rocket leaves, to serve

Makes two 12cm tarts

1. Preheat oven to 150°C and line a tray with baking paper.
2. Cut two circles 12cm in diameter from pastry sheet. Place pastry circles on prepared tray and rest in the refrigerator for at least 30 minutes or preferably overnight.
3. Place tomato halves cut-side up on a separate baking tray. Drizzle with olive oil, sprinkle with herbs and season with salt and pepper. Roast tomatoes in oven for 2 hours, then turn off oven and leave tomatoes to dry in oven overnight.
4. When ready to cook tarts, preheat oven to 200°C. Use a pastry brush to grease two 12cm tart tins with melted butter. Lay tomato halves face down on base of tart tin. Spread a layer of Onion Jam over the tomatoes, then crumble over a layer of goat's cheese.
5. Remove pastry from refrigerator and lay pastry discs over the filling. Bake tarts in centre of oven for 25–30 minutes, or until pastry is golden and crisp.
6. Remove tarts from oven and let stand for 10 minutes before turning out so pastry forms the base of the tart. Garnish with fresh rocket and crumble over extra goat's cheese.

Turkish Pide

This recipe is adapted from one by Dean Brettschneider.
It's a lot easier to make this bread using an electric mixer
with a dough hook, but if you don't have one use your hands.

4 cups high-grade flour

2 tsp salt

1½ tsp instant dry yeast

1 tsp caster sugar

450ml water

2 tsp extra virgin olive oil

1 egg

50ml water

sesame seeds and nigella
seeds, to garnish

Makes 2 loaves

1. In a large bowl, combine flour, salt, yeast, sugar, water and olive oil. Mix with a wooden spoon to form a soft dough. Scrape down sides of bowl, cover with a damp tea towel and leave to stand for 30 minutes.
2. Turn dough by grabbing one side of the dough and folding it into the centre. Turn the bowl 90 degrees and repeat. Do this about eight times. Cover and leave to rest for another 30 minutes.(The dough will be quite sticky, so turning it can be a bit messy.)
3. Repeat the process of turning the dough twice more, resting it for 30 minutes each time.
4. Line two trays with baking paper. Tip dough onto a lightly floured bench, handling it gently to avoid popping air bubbles inside. Cut dough into 2 pieces, place each piece on a baking tray and gently shape into a rectangle. Cover with a damp tea towel and rest for 20 minutes.
5. Preheat oven to 260°C.
6. Whisk egg and 50ml water in a bowl to form an egg wash. Brush a thin layer over top of dough, using a pastry brush. Make indents in top of dough by prodding it evenly down its length with three fingers dipped in egg wash. Sprinkle over sesame and nigella seeds. Rest for 5 minutes.
7. Bake for 6–8 minutes until each loaf is a mottled pale-golden colour.

Chicken and Avocado Sandwiches

Slice 1 loaf Turkish Pide in half lengthways, leaving a hinge, and fold open. Spread ½ cup Aïoli (see page 184) over both sides of cut loaf. Layer 1 cup mesclun leaves over base of loaf, top with slices of Chicken Roulade (see page 12) and slices of avocado. Season with salt and pepper, close sandwich and cut to serve.

little and friday.

Blueberry Poppy Seed Loaf

The complementary flavours of citrus and blueberry make
for an absolute winner.

170g unsalted butter

1 cup caster sugar

1 tsp vanilla extract

zest of 4 lemons

1½ tbsp poppy seeds

pinch of salt

3 eggs

1½ cups flour

1 tsp baking powder

¼ cup milk

1½ cups blueberries, fresh or
frozen

Syrup

4 tbsp lemon juice

4 tbsp caster sugar

Blueberry Icing

2 cups icing sugar

¼ cup fresh blueberries, plus
extra for decorating

Makes 1 loaf

1. Preheat oven to 160°C. Grease and line base and sides of a
   23cm × 13cm loaf tin with baking paper.
2. Using an electric mixer, beat butter and sugar until pale
   and fluffy, scraping down the sides of the bowl as you go.
   Add vanilla, lemon zest, poppy seeds and salt, and mix
   to combine.
3. Add eggs one at a time, making sure each egg is well
   combined before adding the next.
4. In a separate bowl, sift flour and baking powder together
   and stir to combine. Using a metal spoon, fold half the dry
   ingredients into the creamed mixture. Then fold through half
   the milk. Repeat with remaining flour mixture and milk.
5. Spoon a third of the mixture into the prepared loaf tin and
   sprinkle a handful of blueberries over. Repeat until all the
   mixture has been used. Top with remaining blueberries.
6. Bake for 1 hour 10 minutes or until a skewer comes out clean.
7. To make syrup, place lemon juice and sugar in a saucepan
   and heat, stirring, until sugar dissolves. Pour syrup over loaf
   while loaf is still hot. Cool in tin before turning out onto a
   wire rack.
8. To make icing, in a food processor blitz together icing sugar
   and blueberries. Spread icing over cooled loaf, and top with
   extra blueberries.

BIRTHDAY LUNCH

Most ladies love nothing better than to come together, all dressed up, for an elegant birthday celebration. Here, we gathered around the dining table in an airy city loft for a light, relaxed lunch. The recipes can be made a day ahead to allow for maximum ease on the day, and then all you need to do is heat the risotto cakes, toss the salad, and arrange the flowers . . .

Pea and Mint Risotto Cakes

Mushroom Risotto Cakes

Roasted Potato Stacks

Berry Cheesecakes

Gin and Lemon Cake

Pearl Cake

Pea and Mint Risotto Cakes

These savoury cakes are packed with summer flavours.

60g unsalted butter
1 cup finely chopped onion
2 cloves garlic, chopped
1 cup arborio rice
2½ cups chicken or vegetable stock
salt and freshly ground pepper
zest and juice of 1 lemon
2½ cups frozen peas
2 cups fresh mint leaves, torn
6 eggs
½ cup cream
1 cup grated tasty cheese
¾ cup grated Parmesan
¼ cup crumbled feta
¼ cup ricotta
large bunch of basil leaves, roughly torn
400g spinach, chopped

To garnish
9 slices prosciutto
100g goat's cheese
handful of microgreens
6 sugarsnap peas

Makes 6

1. Heat butter in a heavy-based frying pan and gently cook onion and garlic over a low heat until transparent. Do not brown.
2. Add rice and stir continuously for 2 minutes over a medium heat. Meanwhile, heat stock in a saucepan.
3. Add 1 cup of heated stock to rice, stirring constantly until stock has been absorbed. Continue cooking, adding a small amount of stock at a time, until all the stock has been absorbed (around 20 minutes) and risotto is a creamy consistency. Season with salt and pepper and stir in lemon zest and juice. Remove from heat and allow to cool.
4. In a food processor, blitz together frozen peas and mint until puréed.
5. In a large bowl, beat eggs and cream. Add cheeses, basil, spinach and pea purée, and stir to combine. Stir mixture through risotto.
6. Preheat oven to 180°C. Grease and line the base and sides of a 6-hole Texas muffin tray with baking paper.
7. Line the inside of each muffin tin with a slice of prosciutto, then fill with risotto mixture. Bake for 45 minutes or until golden. Remove from oven and cool for 10 minutes before turning out onto a wire rack.
8. To serve, halve remaining prosciutto slices lengthwise. Place a teaspoonful of goat's cheese on one end of each prosciutto slice and roll up to enclose. Top risotto cakes with microgreens, prosciutto rolls and a sugarsnap pea.

Kitchen Notes
Risotto cakes may be made a day in advance and stored in a sealed container in the refrigerator. Remove 1 hour before serving. Reheat for 20 minutes in an oven preheated to 160°C.

Mushroom Risotto Cakes

This is my savoury version of a petit cake.

60g unsalted butter

1 cup finely chopped onion

2 cloves garlic, chopped

¾ cup dried porcini, finely chopped

1 cup arborio rice

2½ cups chicken or vegetable stock

salt and freshly ground pepper

zest and juice of 1 lemon

2 cups sliced button mushrooms

6 eggs

½ cup cream

1 cup grated tasty cheese

¾ cup grated Parmesan

¼ cup crumbled feta

¼ cup fresh ricotta

400g spinach, chopped

large bunch of fresh basil, leaves roughly torn

4 tbsp fresh thyme leaves

To garnish

6 Portobello mushrooms

2 sprigs rosemary leaves, chopped

2 tbsp extra virgin olive oil

3 tsp tomato or basil pesto (we use tomato)

6 tbsp mascarpone

extra sprigs of thyme

Makes 6

1. Heat butter in a heavy-based frying pan and gently cook onion and garlic over a low heat until transparent. Do not brown. Add porcini and cook until soft.

2. Add rice and stir continuously for 2 minutes over a medium heat. Meanwhile, heat stock in a saucepan.

3. Add 1 cup of heated stock to rice, stirring constantly until stock has been absorbed. Continue cooking, adding a small amount of stock at a time, until all the stock has been absorbed (around 20 minutes) and risotto is a creamy consistency.

4. Season to taste with salt and pepper, and stir in lemon zest and juice. Add button mushrooms and stir through mixture to soften. Remove risotto from heat and allow to cool.

5. In a large bowl, beat together eggs and cream. Add cheeses, spinach and herbs, and stir to combine. Stir this mixture through the risotto.

6. Preheat oven to 180°C. Grease and line the base and sides of a 6-hole Texas muffin tray with baking paper. Fill muffin tins with risotto mixture. Bake for 45 minutes or until golden.

7. Remove risotto cakes from oven and cool for 10 minutes before turning out onto a wire rack.

8. Increase oven temperature to 220°C. Place Portobello mushrooms stem-side up on a baking tray, sprinkle with rosemary and drizzle with olive oil. Cover tray tightly with foil and cook for 10 minutes until soft and moist. Allow to cool before using to garnish risotto cakes.

9. To serve, in a bowl mix pesto through mascarpone. Heat a dessertspoon in a glass filled with boiling water, then run the spoon along the surface of the mascarpone at a 45-degree angle to form an egg shape (a quenelle). Lay a quenelle of mascarpone on top of each risotto cake. Be sure to reheat the spoon each time to ensure a perfect, shiny quenelle. Top risotto cakes with a Portobello mushroom and a sprig of thyme.

little and friday.

Roasted Potato Stacks

If you are a cheese-lover, sprinkle grated Parmesan over the stacks just before baking.

5 tbsp extra virgin olive oil

2 cloves garlic, crushed

6 Agria potatoes, peeled

sprig of rosemary, finely chopped

1 tbsp finely chopped thyme leaves

salt and freshly ground pepper

Makes 6

1. Preheat oven to 180°C.
2. Gently heat 3 tablespoons olive oil and the garlic in a small frying pan over a low heat until oil is fragrant but garlic has not browned. Cool.
3. Using a pastry brush, grease a 6-hole Texas muffin tray with the garlic oil.
4. Thinly slice potatoes (use a mandolin slicer if you have one). Place potato slices, rosemary, thyme, salt and pepper and remaining oil into a bowl and toss until potatoes are well coated with the oil and herb mixture.
5. Layer potato slices in muffin tray until full.
6. Bake for 35–45 minutes or until golden. Turn out and serve while still hot.

Berry Cheesecakes

These are best made a day in advance so the topping
has a chance to set.

200g chocolate biscotti
50g unsalted butter
1 punnet strawberries
125g Philadelphia cream cheese
¼ cup caster sugar
½ tsp rosewater
300ml cream
4 leaves gelatine
1 punnet raspberries

Topping
100ml water
¼ cup caster sugar
1 punnet raspberries, plus a few
extra to garnish
2 leaves gelatine
½ cup pomegranate seeds
pansies, borage or violets,
to garnish

Makes 8

1. Grease eight 8cm diameter × 6cm deep metal ring moulds
   and place on a tray lined with baking paper.
2. Place biscotti and butter in a food processor and blitz for
   2 minutes until mixture resembles crumbs. Distribute
   mixture evenly between moulds and, using a glass, press
   mixture firmly to form a solid base.
3. Slice strawberries into 3mm-thick slices and line the sides of
   the moulds, overlapping the slices. Place in the refrigerator
   to chill.
4. Using an electric mixer, beat cream cheese with sugar and
   rosewater until soft and smooth. Turn out into another bowl.
   Pour 250ml cream into mixer bowl and whisk until soft peaks
   form. Fold cream into cream cheese mixture.
5. Meanwhile, soak gelatine in cold water for 2 minutes
   to soften.
6. Pour remaining 50ml cream into a saucepan and heat until
   warm but not boiling. Remove from heat.
7. Remove gelatine from water and squeeze out excess water
   using a clean tea towel. Add gelatine to warm cream and stir
   to dissolve.
8. Mix gelatine and cream into cream cheese mixture. Add
   raspberries and stir to combine.
9. Pour mixture into moulds and refrigerate for 2 hours until set.
10. To make raspberry topping, in a saucepan mix water, sugar
    and raspberries. Simmer for 5 minutes. Remove from heat
    and strain mixture through a sieve. Reserve raspberry syrup.
11. Soak gelatine in water for 2 minutes to soften. Remove and
    squeeze out excess water. Stir gelatine into raspberry syrup.
    Allow to cool slightly before pouring over cheesecakes. Syrup
    shouldn't be so hot that it melts the cheesecake. Refrigerate
    overnight to allow topping to set.
12. When ready to serve, remove cheesecakes from moulds by

running a palette knife soaked in hot water around the inside of the moulds, then gently lifting them off.

13. Decorate cheesecakes with pomegranate seeds, fresh edible flowers and a raspberry. Keep refrigerated until ready to serve.

Kitchen Notes

Ring moulds are available from kitchenware stores.

I use Philadelphia cream cheese because a firm cream cheese is required to ensure the cheesecakes set.

Gin and Lemon Cake

An adaptation of English food writer Jane Grigson's
Gin and Lemon Cake.

250g unsalted butter
1½ cups caster sugar
zest of 6 lemons
4 eggs
2 cups flour
2 tsp baking powder
¾ tsp salt
1½ cups ground almonds
1 cup sour cream

Syrup

¼ cup caster sugar
½ cup water
½ cup lemon juice
6 tbsp gin

Cream Cheese Icing

125g unsalted butter
500g Philadelphia cream
cheese, cubed
1 cup icing sugar, sifted

Makes one 20cm cake

1. Preheat oven to 160°C. Grease a 20cm round cake tin and line bottom and sides with baking paper cut to fit.
2. Using an electric mixer, beat butter, sugar and lemon zest until pale and fluffy. Add eggs one at time, beating well after each addition.
3. Sift flour, baking powder and salt into a bowl. Add ground almonds and mix to combine. Using a large metal spoon, fold dry ingredients into creamed mixture, making sure not to overmix. Add sour cream and stir gently to combine.
4. Spread mixture into prepared tin.
5. Bake cake in centre of oven for 1 hour 50 minutes, or until a skewer comes out clean. Place a baking tray on the top rack of the oven if cake is browning too much.
6. To make syrup, heat sugar, water and lemon juice in a saucepan for approximately 4 minutes until sugar has dissolved. Stir in gin.
7. Remove cake from oven and pour hot syrup over while cake is still hot. Leave for at least 2 hours (refrigerate for the last hour) before icing.

To Assemble

1. To make Cream Cheese Icing, using an electric mixer, beat butter on high speed. Add cream cheese a little at a time, beating on high speed, until completely combined with no lumps (this will take approximately 5 minutes).
2. With mixer on low speed, add sugar and beat until combined.
3. Turn out cake and, using a large serrated knife, slice the top off the cake to create an even surface. Invert cake so the base is now the top, and place on a cake board.
4. Place 3 tablespoons of icing on cake and, using a palette knife, spread the icing evenly to form a thin layer over the top and sides. Place in refrigerator for icing to firm up before repeating with another, thicker, layer of icing.

little and friday.

5. Smooth the icing, using a plastic scraper or a rectangle cut from an ice-cream container. Store the cake in an airtight container in the refrigerator until required. Decorate with fresh flowers.

Kitchen Notes

The icing may be made in advance and stored in an airtight container in the refrigerator for up to two weeks.

Pearl Cake

Another, more skilled, cake-decorating option that
looks beautiful.

1 Gin and Lemon Cake (see page 30)

cornflour, for rolling out

500g ready-to-roll fondant icing

2 tbsp apricot jam

2 tbsp boiling water

2 cups Royal Icing (see below)

15g pearl lustre powder (available from cake decorating suppliers)

1 tbsp gin

fresh flowers, to decorate

Makes one 20cm cake

1. Prepare Gin and Lemon Cake by following the instructions from steps 1 to 7.
2. Turn out cake and, using a serrated knife, slice off the top of the cake to create an even surface. Invert cake so the base is now the top, and place on a cake board.
3. Dust bench with cornflour and roll out fondant icing to form a 30cm-diameter circle approximately 4mm thick.
4. Mix apricot jam with boiling water and paint over cake with a pastry brush to create a glue for the icing.
5. Drape fondant icing over a rolling pin and lay it over the cake. Press icing onto the cake so it sticks, being careful not to drag it down the sides of the cake or it will crack and tear. If this happens, gently rub icing with the palm of your hand to bring it back together. Trim off excess icing using a sharp knife.
6. Use a piping bag with a small (number 3) tip. Half fill the bag with Royal Icing and pipe dots randomly around the base of the cake. Allow to dry for 1–2 minutes, then gently press in the edges to form a pearl shape. Keep building up the layers of pearls until you are happy with the look. Leave to dry for 1–2 hours.
7. Mix pearl lustre powder with gin to form a paste and use a paintbrush to paint the pearls. Decorate cake with fresh flowers.

Royal Icing

Place 3 egg whites and 3 cups sifted icing sugar into the bowl of an electric mixer. Whisk until fluffy and a smooth consistency.
Icing will keep for 3–4 days at room temperature. Makes 2 cups.

Kitchen Notes

Fondant icing is available from cake decorating stores.

Do not refrigerate the cake once iced, as the icing will sweat and become sticky. Keep in a cool place for up to two days.

little and friday.

KIDS' PARTY

When my kids were growing up, I usually avoided food colouring and additives. Parties were the one time that anything went. Throwing a good party is a bit of work and can be exhausting, so make it easy on yourself. We hired a candyfloss machine, because making candyfloss by hand takes hours. A jelly cake can be made using jelly crystals: make it up in a greased bundt tin.

Mini Hot Dogs

Sliders

Donuts

Raspberry Coconut Lamingtons

Pink Lemonade

Toffee Apples

Chocolate Ball Party Cake

Flower Biscuits

Mini Hot Dogs

Hot dogs are a fun savoury offering.

6 beefsteak tomatoes, halved

12 breakfast sausages

12 hot dog buns (see page 183)

4 handfuls mesclun salad leaves

1 recipe Onion Jam (see page 186)

Dijon mustard

Makes 12

1. Preheat oven to 150°C. Place tomato halves cut-side up on a lined baking tray. Drizzle with olive oil and season with salt and freshly ground pepper. Cook for 1½–2 hours.
2. Increase oven to 180°C. Place sausages on a baking tray and cook in the centre of the oven for approximately 20 minutes until golden brown, turning after 10 minutes.
3. Split hot dog buns down the middle and line each with mesclun.
4. Spread 1 tablespoon Onion Jam over salad leaves and place a cooked sausage inside each bun. Top with a dollop of mustard and place a Roasted Tomato on top.

Sliders

Miniature hamburgers – perfect for small people.

2 slices stale white bread

1 onion, finely chopped

600g beef mince

1 carrot, grated

¼ cup grated Parmesan

1 egg

salt and freshly ground pepper

12 slider buns (see page 183)

¼ cup Aïoli (see page 184)

¼ cup tomato sauce

4 handfuls mesclun leaves

12 small slices tasty cheese

3 tomatoes, sliced

Makes 12

1. Toast bread slices on a tray in a 150°C oven for 15 minutes then blitz to fine crumbs in a food processor.
2. Heat 1 tablespoon olive oil in a frying pan and gently fry onion until transparent.
3. In a large bowl, combine mince, carrot, cooked onion, breadcrumbs, Parmesan, egg, salt and pepper.
4. Form mixture into 12 small balls. Flatten to make patties 2cm thick. Refrigerate for 20 minutes until firm.
5. Heat 1 tablespoon olive oil in a frying pan over medium heat. Cook patties on both sides until browned and cooked through.
6. To assemble, split buns and spread each half with Aïoli. Place a cooked patty on the bottom half of each bun and smear with tomato sauce. Top with mesclun, cheese and tomato. Replace top half of the bun and secure with ribbon.

Donuts

Our Little and Friday donuts are legendary. This is my
version for little tummies.

1 recipe Donut Dough (see page 160)

4 cups coconut oil, for frying

2 cups dark compound chocolate buttons

2 cups shredded coconut

2 cups white compound chocolate buttons

Makes approx. 18 small donuts

1. Make Donut Dough by following steps 1–6 on page 160.
2. Use an 8cm-diameter cookie cutter to cut out the donuts. Use a smaller cutter to make a hole in the middle of each one. (You can also use a donut cutter.)
3. Place donuts on a lined baking tray and rest for 20 minutes, until dough feels light and fluffy when pressed.
4. Pour oil into a deep saucepan to 2cm deep. Heat oil to 180°C. If not using a thermometer, heat oil over medium heat – once it starts smoking it is too hot.
5. Drop a few donuts at a time into the hot oil. Do not cook too many at once, or they will stick together. Cook for 2 minutes on each side, until quite dark and crisp.
6. Remove donuts from oil, drain on a wire rack and place on the baking tray to cool.
7. Gently melt dark chocolate in a bowl over a saucepan of simmering water. Dip half the donuts in chocolate then in shredded coconut, and return them to baking tray to dry. Repeat this process with white chocolate for the remaining donuts.

Kitchen Notes

Alternatively, donuts can be dipped in Lemon Icing (page 48) coloured to match your party's theme.

We saved the donut centres and cooked them as above. We then dipped them in Chocolate Ganache (page 187) and rolled them in shredded coconut (see photograph, page 41) and hundreds and thousands (see photograph, page 49).

little and friday.

Raspberry Coconut Lamingtons

Using an apple corer, we cored the centre of the lamingtons
to fill them with fresh cream, topping each with a raspberry.

250g unsalted butter

2½ cups caster sugar

1 tsp vanilla extract

6 eggs

2½ cups flour

2 tsp baking powder

1½ cups shredded coconut

140ml coconut cream

½ cup sour cream

1 cup frozen raspberries, plus
extra to garnish

extra shredded coconut, to coat

whipped cream, to fill

White Chocolate Raspberry Ganache

2 cups cream

1 cup baby marshmallows

2 cups white compound
chocolate buttons

2 cups good-quality white
chocolate buttons

2 tsp freeze-dried raspberry
powder

Makes 30

1. Preheat oven to 180°C. Grease 15 individual 6cm × 4cm baby
   loaf tins and line with baking paper cut to extend 1cm above
   the rims.
2. Using an electric mixer on low speed, beat butter and sugar
   until pale and fluffy. Add vanilla, then add eggs one at a time,
   mixing well after each addition.
3. Sift flour and baking powder into a separate bowl. Add
   shredded coconut and mix to combine.
4. Combine coconut cream and sour cream in a jug.
5. With mixer on low speed, slowly add a third of the dry
   ingredients and a third of the cream mixture. Continue in
   this way until all combined.
6. Spoon a 2cm layer of mixture into each tin. Scatter 4
   raspberries over and continue to fill with cake mixture.
7. Bake in centre of oven for 30–35 minutes or until well risen
   and a skewer comes out clean. Cool before turning out. Cut
   each baby loaf in half to form two squares.
8. To assemble, use a palette knife to thoroughly coat each
   lamington with a thick layer of White Chocolate Raspberry
   Ganache (see below). Roll each cake in shredded coconut.
   Use an apple corer to remove the centres and fill cavity with
   whipped cream. Top with a raspberry.

White Chocolate Raspberry Ganache

Place cream and baby marshmallows in a saucepan and heat
to just below boiling point. Remove from heat and stir in both
measures of white chocolate until smooth. Stir in freeze-dried
raspberry powder. Leave to cool until spreadable.

Kitchen Notes

The ganache is best made the day before you need it.

Freeze-dried raspberry powder is available from specialty food stores.

little and friday.

Pink Lemonade

This has a yummy flavour and looks so pretty in bottles.

Serves 10

4 cups caster sugar
300ml water
100ml freshly squeezed lemon juice
2 litres cranberry juice
1 bunch fresh mint, to garnish
2 cups frozen raspberries, to garnish

1. In a saucepan, heat the sugar and water over low heat to dissolve the sugar.
2. Turn up the heat and bring to the boil. Boil for 2 minutes, then remove from the heat and allow to cool.
3. Add lemon juice to sugar syrup.
4. When ready to serve, pour 50ml sugar syrup per 300ml bottle, and top up with cranberry juice. Garnish with mint leaves and frozen raspberries. Refrigerate remaining sugar syrup for up to a month.

Toffee Apples

Be sure to wash your apples well or the toffee won't stick.

Makes 12

12 golden delicious apples
12 iceblock sticks or wooden chopsticks
4 cups caster sugar
1½ tbsp white vinegar
¾ cup water
1½ tbsp unsalted butter
¾ tsp cream of tartar
red food colouring

1. Wash apples and insert an iceblock stick or cut-down chopstick into the centre of each one. Place on a lined baking tray.
2. In a heavy-based saucepan, combine sugar, vinegar, water, butter and cream of tartar. Heat over a medium heat, stirring slowly, until the sugar has dissolved.
3. Add a few drops of food colouring and mix. Turn up heat and bring mixture to the boil. (Do not stir once it is boiling, as this will make the mixture crystallise.) Boil until the mixture reaches 150°C on a candy thermometer. Turn heat down and simmer for 20 minutes.
4. Remove saucepan from heat and wait until mixture stops bubbling before you begin dipping the apples. You will need to tilt the saucepan to enable a whole apple to be immersed in toffee. Twist the apple around to get a good coating, then place on the baking tray to cool and harden.

little and friday.

Chocolate Ball Party Cake

This festive party cake uses two cake mixes, one flavoured with
cocoa (see page 46) and the other plain vanilla, which is coloured
to make the cake pops placed inside and on top of the cake.
It is best to make the cake pops a day in advance.

3 cups flour
2 tsp baking powder
½ tsp salt
340g unsalted butter
2 cups caster sugar
1 tsp vanilla extract
5 eggs
¾ cup sour cream
orange, green and yellow food
colouring (or use colour gels)

Coloured Cake Pops
Makes 24 cake pops

1. Preheat oven to 190°C. Grease a 12-hole silicone cake-pop
   mould and dust with flour.
2. Sift flour, baking powder and salt into a bowl and stir
   to combine.
3. Using an electric mixer, beat butter and sugar at medium-
   high speed until pale and fluffy. Add vanilla and stir to
   combine.
4. Add eggs one at a time, mixing well after each addition.
5. Using a large spoon, fold dry ingredients through butter
   mixture, then fold in the sour cream.
6. Divide cake mixture among three bowls and add a few
   drops of different food colouring to each bowl. Gently fold
   in colouring.
7. Spoon one bowl of mixture into a piping bag and fill one half
   of each cake-pop mould, then seal the moulds together.
8. Place on a baking tray and bake for 12–15 minutes.
9. Remove from the oven and turn cake pops out onto a wire
   rack. Repeat this process until the different coloured
   mixtures have been used up.

Kitchen Notes

Colour gels give a more vibrant colour. They are available from
specialty cake-decorating stores.

Silicone cake pop moulds are available from specialty kitchenware
stores.

2½ cups flour
½ cup good-quality cocoa
2 tsp baking powder
½ tsp salt
340g unsalted butter
2 cups caster sugar
1 tsp vanilla extract
5 eggs
¾ cup sour cream

To Assemble
24 cake pops (see page 44)
2 cups Chocolate Ganache
(see page 187)
hundreds and thousands

Chocolate Pound Cake
Makes one 18cm double-layer cake

1. Preheat oven to 190°C. Grease two 18cm round cake tins, and line the bottom and sides with baking paper that extends 1cm beyond the edges of the tins.
2. Sift flour, cocoa, baking powder and salt into a bowl and stir to combine.
3. Using an electric mixer, beat butter and sugar at medium-high speed until pale and fluffy. (This will take approximately 5 minutes.) Scrape down sides of bowl. Add vanilla and stir to combine.
4. Add eggs one at a time, mixing well after each addition.
5. Using a large spoon, fold dry ingredients through butter mixture, then fold in the sour cream.
6. Spoon a 2cm layer of mixture into the base of each prepared cake tin. Top with 5–6 different-coloured cake pops. Repeat this process until you run out of cake mix and have used approximately 10–12 cake pops.
7. Bake cakes in centre of oven for 35–40 minutes, or until a skewer comes out clean. Cool before turning out onto wire racks.

To Assemble

1. Using a serrated knife, cut tops off cakes to make them flat. Place one cake on a cake board and, using a palette knife, spread top with a layer of Chocolate Ganache. Place second cake on top, and spread top and sides with a thin layer of ganache. Place cake in refrigerator for 30 minutes.
2. Remove from refrigerator and spread over another thick layer of ganache. Using the palm of your hand, press hundreds and thousands onto the cake until it is completely covered.
3. Cover the extra cake pops with ganache and roll them in hundreds and thousands to cover. Thread onto wooden skewers and insert into the top of the cake.

little and friday.

Flower Biscuits

These are great for adding to party favour bags. The dough
needs to be chilled overnight.

120g unsalted butter
1 cup caster sugar
1 egg
1 tsp vanilla extract
2 cups flour
½ tsp baking powder
pinch of salt

Lemon Icing
1½ cups icing sugar
4 tbsp lemon juice, plus extra
to mix
yellow hundreds and thousands

Makes approx. 20

1. Using an electric mixer, beat butter and sugar until light and
   fluffy. Add egg and vanilla and beat until well combined.
2. Sift flour, baking powder and salt into a separate bowl and
   mix to combine. With the mixer on low speed, slowly add dry
   ingredients to creamed mixture and mix until just combined.
3. Turn dough out onto a floured bench and lightly knead into a
   ball. Wrap in cling film and refrigerate overnight.
4. Remove dough from the refrigerator and lightly knead for
   2 minutes. Place dough between two sheets of baking paper
   and roll out to ½ cm thick. Cut out biscuits with a flower-
   shaped cookie cutter.
5. Using a spatula, carefully transfer the biscuits to two lined
   baking trays. Refrigerate for 20 minutes.
6. Preheat oven to 180°C. Bake biscuits for 12–15 minutes until
   pale golden, rotating trays halfway through.
7. Cool biscuits on a wire rack. When cool, decorate with icing
   and hundreds and thousands.

Lemon Icing

1. Sift icing sugar into a bowl. Add lemon juice a spoonful at a
   time until you have a smooth, thick icing. Spoon the icing
   into a piping bag. Using a small piping nozzle, pipe around
   the petals of each flower shape.
2. Add a little more lemon juice to the icing to make it runnier.
   Pour this mixture into a piping bag and fill in the petal
   outlines on some biscuits.
3. Once icing is dry, pipe a dot of icing into the centre of each
   flower shape and dip into yellow hundreds and thousands.

little and friday.

MOVIE NIGHT

A movie night is a great way to enjoy the company of friends on a balmy summer evening. We set up our movie in a beautiful backyard overlooking Auckland Harbour. We tied a sheet to the trees for a screen and, as the sun went down, snuggled up on old rugs and blankets, sipping hot mulled wine. The food is all quick and easy to prepare, but make the sweets a day ahead.

Caramel Popcorn

Parmesan and Herb Fries

Hot Mulled Wine

Blue Cheese, Prosciutto and Fig Pizza

Ice Cream Sandwiches

Apricot and Plum Jubes

Chocolate Salami

Chewy Caramels

Truffles

Caramel Popcorn

This is a recipe that cannot be made ahead of time, as the
caramel goes tacky after about five hours and it will
stick to your teeth!

10 cups lightly salted plain
popcorn

½ cup blanched almonds,
toasted and chopped

½ cup brown sugar

¼ cup glucose syrup

2 tbsp unsalted butter

1 tsp vanilla extract

½ tsp salt

¼ tsp baking soda

6 medium paper bags, to serve

Makes 6 medium bags

1. Preheat oven to 180°C. Line two trays with baking paper.
2. In a large bowl, mix popcorn with chopped almonds.
3. In a heavy-based saucepan, combine sugar, glucose syrup
   and butter. Bring to the boil and cook over medium heat for
   2 minutes. Do not stir.
4. Remove from heat and whisk in vanilla, salt and baking soda.
   The mixture will puff up when you add the baking soda, so
   work quickly. Pour the caramel over the popcorn and toss
   with a large spoon to coat.
5. Spread coated popcorn over prepared trays and bake for
   2 minutes. Remove from oven and stir to ensure popcorn is
   evenly coated with caramel. Return to the oven for a further
   2 minutes, watching closely to ensure they do not burn.
   Allow to cool and set on trays before filling bags.

Kitchen Notes

To toast almonds, preheat oven to 160°C. Place nuts on a baking tray
and toast for 5–10 minutes.

Parmesan and Herb Fries

My deliciously herby and cheesy version of oven-baked fries.

1kg Agria potatoes, peeled
2 tbsp extra virgin olive oil
3 tbsp finely chopped rosemary
2 tbsp finely chopped fresh thyme or oregano
1 cup grated Parmesan
salt and freshly ground pepper

Serves 4

1. Preheat oven to 220°C. Line two trays with baking paper.
2. Cut potatoes into 1cm-wide fries. Ensure they are a similar thickness so they cook evenly. Place fries in a large bowl and toss with olive oil to coat.
3. Arrange fries in a single layer on prepared baking trays. It is best that they don't touch, to ensure even cooking. Bake for 20 minutes.
4. Remove trays from oven and sprinkle chopped herbs and Parmesan over fries. Season with salt and pepper and toss using a fish slice to coat.
5. Return to oven for a further 15 minutes or until golden. Serve with lashings of your favourite sauce.

Hot Mulled Wine

A warming tumbler of mulled wine is the perfect thing to combat an evening chill in the air.

3 cups water
1 cup caster sugar
rind of 1 lemon
20 whole cloves
2 oranges
3 cinnamon quills
1.5 litres red wine
whole nutmeg, for grating

Makes approx. 2 litres

1. Place water in a saucepan and bring to the boil. Add sugar and bring to the boil again, stirring until dissolved. Add lemon rind, cloves, oranges and cinnamon quills. Boil for 15 minutes.
2. Remove from heat and strain syrup into the top of a double boiler. Add the wine and heat until piping hot but not boiling.
3. Carefully pour into heatproof glasses, and grate a dash of nutmeg over the top before serving.

Blue Cheese, Prosciutto and Fig Pizza

The bases for these pizzas are very thin and crispy.
Try them with all kinds of toppings.

1 pizza base (see page 185)
50g blue cheese
2 fresh figs, sliced
salt and freshly ground pepper
3 tbsp extra virgin olive oil
6 slices prosciutto
50g fresh ricotta
1 bunch basil

Makes one 23cm pizza

1. Preheat oven to 220°C. Line a tray with baking paper and place in oven.
2. Crumble blue cheese over pizza base and top with fig slices. Season with salt and pepper and drizzle with olive oil.
3. Place pizza on preheated tray and bake for 12–15 minutes or until golden and pizza base is crispy. (If using a conventional oven, cook 5 minutes longer.)
4. Garnish with prosciutto slices, crumble ricotta over and scatter with torn basil leaves.

Potato and Rosemary Pizza

Preheat oven to 220°C. Line a tray with baking paper and place in oven. Thinly slice 2 medium peeled potatoes using a mandolin or sharp knife. Cover a 23cm pizza base with overlapping slices of potato. Sprinkle over a little chopped rosemary. Season with salt and pepper and drizzle with 3 tablespoons olive oil. Place pizza on preheated tray and bake for 12–15 minutes or until golden and pizza base is crispy. (If using a conventional oven, cook 5 minutes longer.) Tear 4 bocconcini into pieces and scatter over pizza before serving. Makes one 23cm pizza.

Zucchini Flower Pizza

Preheat oven to 220°C. Line a tray with baking paper and place in oven. Top a 23cm pizza base with 1 large or 2 small thinly sliced zucchini and 50g crumbled goat's cheese. Tear up 2 zucchini flowers and scatter over. Season with salt and pepper and drizzle with 3 tablespoons olive oil. Place pizza on preheated tray and bake for 12–15 minutes or until golden and pizza base is crispy. (If using a conventional oven, cook 5 minutes longer.) Top with 1 bunch torn basil leaves. Makes one 23cm pizza.

Ice Cream Sandwiches

This recipe makes more than enough ice cream, so you will
have some left over for another day.

28 Chocolate Biscuits
(see below)

Ice Cream

4 eggs, separated

¾ cup caster sugar

1½ cups cream

½ cup freeze-dried mandarin
segments, finely chopped

½ cup grated good-quality dark
chocolate

Makes 14

1. To make ice cream, using an electric mixer, whisk egg whites
   until stiff peaks form. Add ½ cup sugar and beat a further
   4 minutes. Remove to another bowl.
2. In a separate bowl, beat egg yolks and remaining ¼ cup sugar
   until thick and creamy.
3. Whisk cream in electric mixer until stiff.
4. Fold beaten egg whites and cream through egg yolk mixture
   with a metal spoon. Fold chopped mandarin and grated
   chocolate through mixture.
5. Pour into a 2-litre plastic container, cover and freeze for
   6 hours.
6. Just before serving, remove ice cream from freezer and
   cut into 14 slices 2cm thick. Sandwich between chocolate
   biscuits and tie with a ribbon. Return to the freezer briefly
   before serving.

Chocolate Biscuits

Preheat oven to 160°C and line two trays with baking paper.
On a floured bench roll out 1 recipe Chocolate Cookie Dough
(see page 187) to 3mm thick. Using a 7cm-diameter cookie cutter
(we used one with a scalloped edge) cut out 28 circles and place
on prepared trays. Bake for 12–15 minutes. Cool on a wire rack
before assembling. Makes 28 biscuits.

Kitchen Notes

Freeze-dried mandarins are available at specialty food stores.

Baked cookies may be stored in an airtight container for up to
one week.

Apricot and Plum Jubes

The flavour of these sweets is really intense and zingy,
thanks to the fresh fruit used in their making.

550ml Apricot or Plum Purée
(see below), or use storebought
purée
¼ cup passionfruit juice
1 cup caster sugar
½ cup glucose syrup
1 tbsp lemon juice
12 gelatine leaves
1 cup icing sugar
1 cup cornflour

Apricot or Plum Purée
14 medium to large plums
or apricots
¼ cup caster sugar
juice of 3 oranges

Makes approx. 40

1. Grease and line a 20cm-square cake tin with baking paper.
2. In a saucepan, combine fruit purée, passionfruit juice, sugar and glucose syrup and place over medium heat. Stir to prevent the mixture catching on the bottom of the pan, and bring to the boil.
3. Turn heat to high and boil for 10 minutes until mixture thickens and becomes translucent. Add lemon juice and cook for a further 1 minute.
4. Cover gelatine leaves with cold water and leave to stand for 5 minutes to soften. Drain, squeezing out any excess water with a clean tea towel. Add gelatine to hot fruit mixture. Whisk well to combine.
5. Pour into prepared tin and place in the refrigerator overnight to set. Once set, turn out onto a piece of baking paper.
6. Sift together icing sugar and cornflour and stir to combine. Cut jubes into 2cm squares and roll in sugar mixture.

Apricot or Plum Purée
To make purée, preheat oven to 150°C. Halve plums or apricots and remove stones. Place fruit face down in an oven dish. Sprinkle with sugar and squeeze the orange juice over. Cook for 30 minutes. Cool, then purée fruit and juice in a food processor.

Kitchen Notes
Jubes will keep for two weeks in an airtight container at room temperature.

Chocolate Salami

This is a super-easy, no-bake treat.

250g Super Wine biscuits
2 eggs
½ cup caster sugar
110g unsalted butter
1 cup good-quality cocoa
100g good-quality dark chocolate, chopped
½ cup pistachios
½ cup dried pears, finely chopped
3 tbsp Stone's Green Ginger Wine
½ cup icing sugar

Makes approx. 20

1. Blitz biscuits in a food processor until fine crumbs form.
2. Put eggs and sugar in a bowl over a saucepan of simmering water. Whisk until the sugar has dissolved and the mixture has thickened.
3. Add butter, ½ cup cocoa and chocolate and whisk for 2 minutes or until smooth. Remove from heat and stir in biscuit crumbs, pistachios, dried pears and wine.
4. Turn mixture out onto a sheet of cling film and roll into a thin log. Wrap and refrigerate overnight.
5. To serve, mix together remaining ½ cup cocoa and icing sugar in a shallow dish. Unwrap Chocolate Salami and roll in cocoa mix. Cut into 1cm slices and serve in mini patty cases.

Chewy Caramels

Caramels will keep for two weeks in an airtight container.

2½ cups caster sugar
50ml water
100g unsalted butter
150ml golden syrup
500ml cream
1 tsp salt
½ tsp vanilla extract

Makes approx. 40 pieces

1. Grease and line a 20cm square cake tin with baking paper.
2. Combine half the sugar and the water in a heavy-based saucepan and place over medium heat. Cook until mixture starts to turn golden. Remove from heat and add butter, remaining sugar, golden syrup and cream.
3. Bring to the boil, brushing down the sides of the saucepan with a wet pastry brush to prevent mixture crystallising. Do not stir once mixture starts boiling. Cook until the temperature reaches 122°C when tested with a candy thermometer (approximately 12 minutes).
3. Remove from heat and stir in salt and vanilla. Pour into prepared tin and cool for approximately 6 hours.
4. Cut into 5cm × 2cm pieces and wrap in greaseproof paper.

little and friday.

Truffles

Rich, dark and decadent, these are the ultimate
celebratory treat.

⅔ cup cream

30ml espresso coffee or 1 tbsp
instant coffee

180g good-quality dark
chocolate, chopped

2 tsp unsalted butter

1 tbsp Frangelico liqueur

180g good-quality dark
chocolate, for dipping

¼ cup good-quality cocoa,
to dust

Makes 24 truffles

1. Place cream and coffee in a saucepan over medium heat and
   bring to the boil.
2. Remove from heat and stir in chocolate.
3. Stir in butter and Frangelico liqueur until smooth. Allow to
   set overnight or until firm.
4. When you are ready to make the truffles, melt the second
   measure of chocolate in a bowl over a saucepan of simmering
   water, being careful not to let the bowl touch the hot water or
   the chocolate will seize and it will not melt. (If this happens,
   throw it away and start again – there is no saving it.) When
   melted, put aside to thicken a little for 5 minutes while you
   roll the truffles.
5. Scoop out teaspoonfuls of truffle mixture and, using your
   hands, roll each into a ball.
6. Dip each ball in melted chocolate, tapping the truffle on the
   side of the bowl to get rid of excess chocolate. Place on a
   lined tray and allow the chocolate to firm slightly. Before the
   chocolate sets, roll in cocoa powder and place on another
   lined tray to set.

CHRISTMAS

Christmas in my family has always been a day of sharing simple, fresh food – and far too much sweet, rich food – then lying around, sleeping it all off. Here, I have included my family's Christmas staples such as the Chocolate Roulade and my mum's pav; some simple salads; and traditional favourites such as baked ham and steamed pudding. Finally, as a gift idea, you'll find a collection of biscuit recipes for a Christmas sampler box.

Zucchini Salad

Panzanella

Christmas Ham

Summer Pavlova

Chocolate Roulade

Strawberry Tart

Christmas Pudding

Christmas Mince Tarts

Cookie Sampler Box

Zucchini Salad

Home-grown zucchini flowers give this simple salad a visual lift.

4 yellow and 4 green zucchini
1 handful fresh basil leaves
8 large mint leaves
4 zucchini flowers
juice of 1 lemon
2 tbsp extra virgin olive oil
salt and freshly ground pepper
1 cup shaved pecorino cheese

Serves 6–8

1. Shred zucchini into ribbons using a vegetable peeler or mandolin. Place in a salad bowl.
2. Roughly tear up herbs and zucchini flowers and toss through zucchini.
3. Combine lemon juice, olive oil, salt and pepper, then drizzle over salad.
4. Sprinkle with pecorino shavings and gently toss.

Panzanella

A salad to celebrate tomato season.

½ loaf day-old crusty bread
2 tbsp extra virgin olive oil
salt and freshly ground pepper
1kg mixed tomatoes, halved
3 tbsp red wine vinegar
¼ cup extra virgin olive oil
1 red onion, finely sliced
1 clove garlic, crushed
1 cup fresh basil leaves

Dressing
2 anchovies
1 tbsp capers
2 cloves garlic
6 basil leaves
3 tbsp extra virgin olive oil

Serves 6–8

1. To make croûtons, preheat oven to 200°C and line a tray with baking paper. Tear bread into 3cm pieces and place on tray. Drizzle with 2 tablespoons olive oil, season with salt and pepper and toss to coat. Bake for 10–12 minutes, or until golden brown and crunchy. Cool.
2. In a large bowl, gently toss together tomatoes, vinegar, olive oil, onion and garlic. Season with salt and freshly ground pepper. Allow mixture to rest for at least 10 minutes.
3. Toss croûtons through salad. Leave to rest for approximately 15 minutes.
4. Pound together dressing ingredients in a mortar and pestle and season with salt and freshly ground pepper.
5. Transfer salad to a platter, scatter with torn basil leaves and drizzle with dressing. Serve immediately.

little and friday.

Christmas Ham

There is nothing better than ham at Christmas. Afterwards,
our family always took the leftover ham away with us for
sandwiches on a camping trip.

8kg leg of ham
30–40 whole cloves
½ cup Dijon mustard
300ml maple syrup
100ml fresh orange juice
salt and freshly ground pepper

Serves 10–12, with leftovers

1. Preheat oven to 180°C and line a large baking dish with
   baking paper.
2. Using your hands, gently peel back skin from ham to the
   thinnest part of the leg, leaving behind the layer of fat. Use a
   sharp knife to score the skin around the leg. Remove the skin
   in a single piece and discard.
3. Using a sharp knife, score diagonal lines in the fat to create
   a diamond pattern. Insert a whole clove in the centre of each
   diamond, or, if you prefer, where the diamonds intersect.
4. In a bowl, combine mustard, maple syrup and orange juice.
   Season to taste with salt and pepper.
5. Place ham on prepared dish and brush with half the glaze.
   Cook for 1 hour, brushing frequently with remaining glaze
   until a deep golden colour.

Summer Pavlova

This is my mother's easy recipe. It can be made two days before you need it and dressed on the day.

6 egg whites, at room temperature
pinch of salt
2 cups caster sugar
2 tsp cornflour
1½ tsp malt vinegar
1½ tsp vanilla extract

Cherry Coulis

1 cup fresh cherries, pitted
2 tbsp caster sugar
4 tbsp water

To Assemble

500ml cream
¼ cup icing sugar, sifted
½ tsp vanilla extract
1 punnet fresh raspberries
1 punnet fresh blackberries
2 punnets fresh strawberries
500g fresh cherries

Makes one 23cm pavlova

1. Preheat oven to 150°C. Line a tray with baking paper. Using a pencil, draw around a 23cm cake tin on the baking paper to make an outline for your pavlova. Turn the paper over so the pencil line is on the back of the paper.
2. Using an electric mixer, whisk egg whites with salt at high speed until they are white and fluffy and soft peaks form. Add sugar a tablespoon at a time, making sure each spoonful is well combined before adding the next. This will take approximately 10 minutes. The mixture should have a sheen, and be smooth with no lumps.
3. Sprinkle cornflour, vinegar and vanilla over meringue and fold through gently with a large metal spoon. Pile mixture onto prepared baking tray, spreading lightly into the shape of the circle.
4. Bake in centre of oven for 50 minutes. Turn off oven but do not open oven door. Leave pavlova in oven overnight to dry and form a crisp crust.
5. To make Cherry Coulis, place ingredients in a saucepan and cook over medium heat for 15 minutes. Cool before using.
6. To assemble, beat cream until fluffy. Sprinkle icing sugar and vanilla over cream and beat to combine. Spread onto pavlova and decorate with fruit. Drizzle with Cherry Coulis.

Coffee and Cherry Pavlova

Make pavlova as above, but add 1 teaspoon natural coffee extract or 50ml strong espresso, cooled, to mixture at step 3 in place of vanilla. You can also add coffee extract or a little cooled espresso to the cream.

Kitchen Notes

If the pavlova oozes syrup, it needs a little more cooking; if golden-coloured sugar crystals form on the crust, it is overcooked.

little and friday.

Chocolate Roulade

Oh-so-rich, and always a Christmas standout.

Sponge
5 eggs
½ cup caster sugar
1 tsp vanilla
½ cup flour
½ cup good-quality cocoa
½ tsp baking powder
2 cups cream
4 cups Chocolate Ganache
(see page 187)
1 cup fresh cherries, pitted
and chopped, plus extra whole
cherries, to garnish
Chocolate Leaves (see below)

Coulis
2 cups frozen raspberries
½ cup caster sugar
2 tbsp water

Chocolate Leaves
1 cup chocolate melts
20 camellia leaves

Makes one 25cm roulade

1. Preheat oven to 160°C and line a 36cm × 25cm sponge roll tin with baking paper.
2. Using an electric mixer, whisk eggs, sugar and vanilla for 5 minutes until thick and creamy and the mixture forms ribbon trails when you lift the beater.
3. In a separate bowl, sift flour, cocoa and baking powder and mix to combine.
4. Using a large metal spoon, fold dry ingredients through egg mixture until combined. Spread mixture into prepared tin.
5. Bake for 15 minutes or until the top of the sponge springs back when lightly touched.
6. Turn out onto a clean tea towel and cool for 2 minutes. While sponge is still warm, with long side facing you, roll it up in the tea towel into a log. Leave to cool completely.
7. To make coulis, place berries, sugar and water in a saucepan over medium heat and cook for 6–8 minutes. Cool.
8. Whisk 2 cups cream until soft peaks form and fold into 2 cups Chocolate Ganache. Gently unroll the sponge and spread with the ganache mixture. (If sponge cracks, repair with extra ganache.) Top with coulis and chopped cherries. Roll up to enclose filling.
9. Place log on a wire rack with a tray underneath. Pour 1 cup Chocolate Ganache over, until the log is well covered. Leave to set for 2 hours, then repeat with remaining ganache. Garnish with Chocolate Leaves and cherries.

Chocolate Leaves

1. Place chocolate melts in a glass bowl over a saucepan of simmering water and gently melt.
2. Using a paintbrush, paint melted chocolate onto camellia leaves. Once dry, gently peel leaf off chocolate. Use a palette knife to ease them apart if necessary. Glue any broken Chocolate Leaves together by painting chocolate on the underside of the leaf.

little and friday.

Strawberry Tart

This festive tart is also delicious made with sliced mango in place of strawberries.

1 recipe Sweet Pastry (see page 182)

Filling

4 cups Crème Pâtissière (see page 188)

3 cups frozen raspberries

1½ cups Crème Diplomat (see page 189)

2 punnets strawberries, sliced

icing sugar, for dusting

Makes one 28cm tart

1. Line a 28cm tart tin with baking paper cut to fit.
2. On a lightly floured bench, roll out pastry to 3mm thick and line tart tin, making sure to press pastry into edges of tin. Rest pastry case in the refrigerator for 20 minutes.
3. Preheat oven to 180°C. Fill pastry case with Crème Pâtissière and scatter raspberries over. Place filled tart tin on a baking tray and bake for 50 minutes, or until pastry is golden. Allow to cool completely before removing from tin.
4. When ready to serve, cover tart with Crème Diplomat. Arrange layers of sliced strawberries over tart as pictured. Dust with sifted icing sugar.

Kitchen Notes

When transferring pastry to line a tart tin, drape the pastry over a rolling pin. Then roll it back off the rolling pin and lay over the tin. Gently press into the tin to line the base and edges.

You will need to make a double batch of Crème Pâtissière for this recipe.

Christmas Pudding

When I was young, my mum used to put a sixpence in the
pudding mix; the person who found it in their pudding got to
make a special wish. These days you can add a dollar coin or
an old 5-cent piece, wrapped in foil.

Pudding

1 cup raisins, chopped
1 cup pitted prunes, chopped
½ cup fresh dates, chopped
½ cup dried pears, chopped
½ cup currants
¼ cup dried figs, chopped
¼ cup dried apricots, chopped
zest and juice of 1 lemon
zest and juice of 1 orange
1 cup sherry
200g unsalted butter
2 cups brown sugar
3 eggs
1 green apple, peeled and grated
1 cup flour
1 cup fresh breadcrumbs
1 cup ground almonds
1 tbsp cinnamon
2 tsp ground ginger
½ tsp freshly grated nutmeg
2 tsp mixed spice
pinch of salt
1 tsp baking powder
2 tbsp milk
100ml rum or brandy
Rum Sauce (see opposite),
to serve
10 fresh figs, quartered, to serve

Serves 10–12

1. In a large mixing bowl, combine dried fruit, lemon and
   orange zest and juice, and sherry. Soak overnight (or for up
   to one week), stirring occasionally. The longer you leave it,
   the better.
2. Grease a large pudding steamer or basin.
3. Using an electric mixer, cream butter and sugar until pale
   and fluffy. Scrape down sides of bowl, then beat for a further
   minute.
4. Add eggs one a time, making sure each egg is well combined
   before adding the next.
5. In a large bowl, combine apple, flour, breadcrumbs, ground
   almonds, spices, salt and baking powder. Add soaked fruit
   and stir to combine. Add creamed mixture with milk and
   rum or brandy and combine.
6. Spoon mixture into prepared pudding steamer or basin to
   fill. Lay a piece of baking paper on top and secure with lid. If
   you don't have a pudding steamer, top with two pieces of foil
   large enough to overhang edges of basin. Secure with string
   tied around the top rim of the basin.
7. Place pudding into a saucepan and add boiling water to just
   below the top rim of the basin. Simmer for 5 hours, topping
   up from time to time with boiling water.
8. Remove from water and let stand for 10 minutes before
   turning out.
9. To serve, pour Rum Sauce over pudding, and serve extra
   sauce in a jug on the side. Decorate with fresh figs.

little and friday.

55g unsalted butter
¾ cup flour
¾ cup milk
¾ cup caster sugar
5 tbsp dark rum

Rum Sauce

1. Melt butter in a saucepan over medium heat. Add flour and stir with a wooden spoon until golden, approximately 2 minutes. Slowly add milk and whisk until thick and smooth. Add sugar and whisk until dissolved.
2. Lower heat and cook for 5 minutes, stirring with a wooden spoon. Add rum and stir to combine.

Kitchen Notes

The cooked pudding may be made up to four weeks ahead and stored in the pudding basin in a cool, dark place. When ready to serve, heat in a saucepan of simmering water for 1 hour. Rum Sauce may be made a day ahead and refrigerated. Simply reheat when required.

Christmas Mince Tarts

Christmas just isn't complete without mince tarts.

Fruit Mince

1½ cups raisins

1½ cups sultanas

1½ cups currants

¾ cup dried figs

¾ cup dried pears

2 Granny Smith apples, peeled and grated

½ tsp ground cloves

½ tsp freshly grated nutmeg

1 tsp mixed spice

2 tbsp manuka honey

1 cup brown sugar

zest and juice of 1 orange

zest and juice of 1 lemon

½ cup verjuice or brandy

extra ¼ cup brandy, or more if required

1 double recipe Sweet Pastry (see page 182)

icing sugar, for dusting

Makes 48 mini tarts

1. In a food processor, blitz dried fruit until chopped.
2. Place all ingredients except extra brandy in a large airtight container and stir to combine.
3. Cover and soak for one week (or up to three months), adding the extra brandy to keep mixture moist. Stir at regular intervals. When ready to use, you can lightly pulse the mixture in a food processor to create a finer mince.
4. To make tarts, preheat oven to 180°C.
5. On a lightly floured bench, roll out pastry to 3mm thick. Using an 8cm-diameter cookie cutter, cut out 24 circles. Line two 12-hole mini muffin trays with pastry, trimming each to form a neat edge.
6. Rest uncooked pastry cases in refrigerator for 20 minutes. Fill each case with 2 teaspoons fruit mince. Roll out remaining pastry and cut out stars or other shapes for tops.
7. Bake for 20 minutes or until pastry is golden. Cool before removing from tins. Repeat steps 5–7 for next batch of tarts. Dust with icing sugar to serve.

Chocolate Stamped Biscuits

We make thousands of these in our stores at Christmas. To get the
beautiful stamp effect, use any Christmas-themed stamp.

1 recipe Chocolate Cookie Dough
(see page 187)

Makes approx. 30

1. Line two trays with baking paper.
2. Lightly knead cookie dough for 2 minutes. Place between two
   sheets of baking paper and roll out to 5mm thick.
3. Using an 8cm-diameter cookie cutter with a frilled edge,
   cut out approximately 30 rounds. Place on baking trays,
   decorate with a cookie stamp and refrigerate for 20 minutes.
4. Preheat oven to 180°C and bake biscuits for 10–12 minutes.
   Cool on baking trays.

Chocolate Coconut Fingers

My versatile Chocolate Cookie Dough is transformed with a
melted chocolate and coconut coating.

1 recipe Chocolate Cookie Dough
(see page 187)

900g good-quality chocolate,
chopped

8 cups shredded coconut

Makes approx. 50

1. Line two trays with baking paper.
2. Lightly knead cookie dough for 2 minutes. Place between two
   sheets of baking paper and roll out to 1cm thick.
3. Cut dough into 12cm × 1cm strips. Roll into cigar shapes and
   place on baking trays. Refrigerate for 20 minutes.
4. Preheat oven to 180°C and bake biscuits for 12–15 minutes.
   Cool before icing.
5. To make icing, melt chocolate in a glass bowl over a saucepan
   of simmering water, stirring until smooth. Dip biscuits in
   chocolate to coat completely. Roll in coconut and place on
   baking paper to set.

little and friday.

Pear Russian Teacakes

These traditional Christmas cookies are also known as
Mexican wedding cookies. You can substitute almonds or
walnuts for the macadamia nuts.

1½ cups macadamia nuts
225g unsalted butter
½ cup icing sugar
1 egg yolk
1 tsp vanilla extract
2½ cups plain flour
¼ tsp cinnamon
¼ tsp grated nutmeg
¼ tsp ground ginger
pinch of salt
35–40 cloves
2 cups icing sugar

Makes 35–40

1. Preheat oven to 180°C. Line two trays with baking paper.
2. Place nuts in a food processor and blitz until a fine meal consistency is reached.
3. Using an electric mixer, beat butter and first measure of icing sugar until light and fluffy. Add egg yolk and vanilla and mix to combine.
4. Using a large metal spoon, fold ground nuts, flour, ground spices and salt through creamed mixture until well combined.
5. Roll tablespoonfuls of mixture into balls, then form each ball into a pear shape. Push a clove into the top of each one for the stalk as pictured. Place 2cm apart on prepared baking trays and bake for 20 minutes or until light golden.
6. Remove from oven and dust with icing sugar while still hot. When cool, dust the teacakes with icing sugar a second time before serving.

Citrus Spice Cookies

These biscuits have a real tang from the pomegranate molasses.

2½ cups flour
1 tsp baking soda
1½ tsp each ground cinnamon, nutmeg, cloves, ginger
¼ tsp each salt, pepper
200g unsalted butter
⅓ cup brown sugar
1 egg yolk
1 tsp vanilla extract
3 tbsp pomegranate molasses
¼ cup golden syrup
½ cup caster sugar
½ cup demerara sugar
1 tsp grated lemon zest
1 tsp grated orange zest

Makes approx. 30

1. Preheat oven to 190°C and line two trays with baking paper.
2. In a mixing bowl combine flour, baking soda and spices, including salt and pepper. Stir with a whisk to aerate.
3. Using an electric mixer, cream butter and brown sugar until pale and fluffy. Scrape down sides of bowl and beat a further minute. Add egg yolk and vanilla and beat to combine.
4. Stir in pomegranate molasses and golden syrup. Fold flour and spices through to combine.
5. In a separate bowl, combine caster sugar, demerara sugar and lemon and orange zest.
6. Using damp hands, form tablespoonfuls of dough into balls. Roll in sugar and zest mix. Place 5cm apart on trays and lightly press down with your fingers, but do not flatten.
7. Bake for 10 minutes or until the tops crack. Cool on a rack.

Peppermint Creams

These are best enjoyed with a strong coffee.

1 recipe Chocolate Cookie Dough (see page 187)
4 cups icing sugar, sifted
2 egg whites
3 drops peppermint oil

Makes approx. 25

1. Lightly knead cookie dough for 2 minutes. Place between two sheets of baking paper and roll out to 5mm thick. Using a 6cm-diameter cookie cutter, cut out 50 rounds. Place on lined baking trays and refrigerate for 20 minutes.
2. Preheat oven to 180°C and bake biscuits for 12–15 minutes. Cool before icing.
3. To make peppermint icing, using an electric mixer whisk icing sugar and egg whites until firm. Mix in peppermint oil.
4. Sandwich biscuits together using 1 tablespoon peppermint icing. Leave overnight so icing becomes firm.

little and friday.

Salted Caramel Biscuits

This is my version of a Tim Tam biscuit, filled with a salty, gooey caramel.

4 cups caster sugar

600ml cream

½ tsp salt (and more to taste)

1 recipe Chocolate Cookie Dough (see page 187)

900g good-quality dark chocolate, chopped

Makes approx. 30

1. To make caramel, place sugar in a heavy-based saucepan and just cover with water to achieve a wet sand consistency. Bring to the boil but do not stir. Using a wet pastry brush, carefully clean sides of saucepan to remove any stray sugar crystals. Continue to boil until sugar turns a rich amber colour. Quickly remove from heat.

2. In another small saucepan, heat cream to boiling point. Gradually add hot cream to caramelised sugar, stirring constantly until smooth. Add salt to taste (the caramel should taste salty). Set aside to cool and thicken.

3. Line two trays with baking paper.

4. Remove cookie dough from refrigerator and lightly knead for 2 minutes. Place between two sheets of baking paper and roll out to 5mm thick.

5. Using a sharp knife, cut dough into 12cm × 3cm rectangles. Transfer to baking trays with a spatula and refrigerate for 20 minutes.

6. Preheat oven to 180°C and bake biscuits for 10–12 minutes. Cool before icing.

7. Transfer caramel to a piping bag and pipe a wide strip down the centre of each biscuit. Leave to set.

8. Melt chocolate in a glass bowl over a saucepan of simmering water, stirring until smooth. Allow to cool for 5 minutes before dipping the top of each biscuit in chocolate to coat. Work quickly so the caramel doesn't melt. Transfer remaining chocolate to a piping bag and pipe thin stripes lengthwise onto biscuits to decorate. (Pictured page 87, bottom right.)

Chocolate Nut Biscuit Bars

A chocolate and nut coating makes these simple biscuits irresistible.

1 recipe Chocolate Cookie Dough (see page 187)

400g unsalted butter

¼ cup caster sugar

½ cup honey

1 cup cream

5 cups hazelnuts, roasted and roughly chopped

180g good-quality dark chocolate, chopped

Makes approx. 30

1. Line two trays with baking paper.
2. Remove cookie dough from refrigerator and lightly knead for 2 minutes. Place between two sheets of baking paper and roll out to 5mm thick.
3. Using a sharp knife, cut dough into 12cm × 3cm rectangles. Transfer to prepared baking trays and refrigerate for 20 minutes.
4. Preheat oven to 180°C and bake biscuits for 12–15 minutes. Leave to cool on baking trays while you prepare nut topping.
5. To make nut topping, place butter, sugar, honey and cream in a saucepan and bring to the boil. Add nuts and cook over a medium heat for a further 5 minutes, or until golden.
6. Spoon nut mixture over cooked biscuits and bake for a further 10 minutes, until golden. Cool before icing.
7. Melt chocolate in a glass bowl over a saucepan of simmering water, stirring until smooth. Put chocolate in a piping bag fitted with a fine nozzle and pipe zigzag stripes over the biscuits. (Pictured page 87, top right.)

Kitchen Notes

To roast hazelnuts, preheat oven to 160°C. Place nuts on a baking tray and roast for 10 minutes. Remove skins by rubbing in a tea towel.

Shrewsbury Biscuits

My wonderfully buttery version of a favourite tea-time treat.
You can vary the sizes, and a small biscuit stacked on top of a
large biscuit looks extra pretty.

240g unsalted butter

2 cups caster sugar

2 eggs

2 tsp vanilla extract

4 cups flour

1 tsp baking powder

pinch of salt

icing sugar, to dust

Raspberry Filling

4 cups frozen raspberries

1 cup caster sugar

zest and juice of 1 lemon

Makes approx. 14 biscuits

1. Using an electric mixer, beat butter and sugar until pale and fluffy. Scrape down sides of bowl, then beat for 1 further minute. Add eggs, mixing well after each addition. Add vanilla and mix to combine.
2. In a separate bowl, combine flour, baking powder and salt. Using a large metal spoon, fold flour through creamed mixture until combined. Turn dough out onto a lightly floured bench and gently work with your hands to form a ball. Wrap in cling film and refrigerate for 1 hour.
3. Preheat oven to 180°C. Line two trays with baking paper.
4. On a lightly floured bench, roll out dough to 3mm thick and cut out 28 rounds using an 8cm-diameter cookie cutter. Place 2cm apart on prepared baking trays. To form the tops, use a 3cm-diameter cookie cutter to cut out the centres from 14 rounds.
5. Bake for 10 minutes or until lightly golden. Cool before assembling.
6. To make Raspberry Filling, combine raspberries, sugar, zest and juice in a heavy-based saucepan and stir over a low heat. Increase heat and bring to the boil, then reduce heat and simmer for 30–35 minutes until thick. Cool before using.
7. Spread filling onto bases and seal with tops. Dust with icing sugar.

Kitchen Notes

Cookies will keep for one week in an airtight container.

For the photograph, we made a double batch of dough and used a 6cm-diameter cutter to create the smaller Shrewsbury Biscuits.

WEDDING

There is something to be said for a simple wedding. For this occasion, we hired the local Sea Scouts' hall so our wonderful barista Tomas and his beautiful wife Andreas could renew their vows. We served easy, tasty bites with beers in the afternoon sun and, as the evening wore on, everyone assembled for a classic white dessert banquet.

Tomato and Olive Bruschetta

Potato Galettes

Fig Galettes

Chocolate Meringue Cakes

Pistachio Nougat

Lime Meringue Tartlets

Kaffir Lime and Coconut Brûlées

Meringue Kisses

White Chocolate and Berry Mousse

Cardamom and White Chocolate Wedding Cake

Passionfruit and Yoghurt Wedding Cake

Tomato and Olive Bruschetta

These can be eaten hot or cold. Make the Brioche Dough the
day before and finish off the bruschetta on the day.

½ recipe Brioche Dough (see page 184)

1 bulb Roasted Garlic (see page 186)

2kg (approx. 100) small vine-ripened tomatoes

extra virgin olive oil

salt and freshly ground pepper

150g olive tapenade

1½ cups grated Parmesan

1 handful thyme leaves, chopped, plus extra sprigs to garnish

12 slices prosciutto, torn

250g feta

2 cups Kalamata olives

Makes 50 small bruschetta

1. Cut Brioche Dough in two. On a floured bench, roll each piece out to 3mm thick. Place on lined baking trays, cover with baking paper and refrigerate for 2 hours.
2. On a floured bench, roll each sheet of dough out to 1mm thick – the thinner, the better. Rest for 10 minutes. Using a sharp knife, cut each dough sheet into approximately 25 rectangles. Place on lined baking trays.
3. Preheat oven to 150°C.
4. Squeeze garlic out of skins and smear over prepared dough.
5. Cut tomatoes in half and place cut-side up on a lined baking tray. Drizzle with olive oil and season with salt and pepper. Bake for 30 minutes.
6. Increase oven temperature to 180°C.
7. Top each rectangle of dough with olive tapenade, a sprinkling of Parmesan and chopped thyme leaves. Bake for 10 minutes or until golden. Cool.
8. Top each bruschetta with tomato halves, prosciutto pieces, crumbled feta and an olive. Drizzle with extra oil and season with salt and pepper. Garnish with thyme sprigs.

Tomato and Mozzarella Bruschetta

As a topping variation, follow steps 1–4 above. Sprinkle with 1½ cups grated Parmesan and bake for 10 minutes or until golden. Cool, then scatter over 2kg (approximately 100) small vine-ripened tomatoes, diced and drained, 250g torn buffalo mozzarella and 1 bunch torn basil leaves. Drizzle with extra virgin olive oil and season with salt and pepper.

Potato Galettes

The pastry can be made the day before and the galettes
cooked just before serving.

2 sheets Flaky Pastry (see
page 182)

Topping

50 baby new potatoes, thinly
sliced with a mandolin

4 tbsp extra virgin olive oil

8 sprigs rosemary, finely
chopped

4 cloves garlic, crushed

2 cups grated Parmesan

2 cups Rocket Pesto (see
page 185)

2 cups fresh rocket

5–8 bocconcini, torn into small
pieces

1 cup Balsamic Reduction
(see page 185)

salt and freshly ground pepper

Egg Wash

2 eggs

2 tbsp cream

Makes approx. 60 petites galettes

1. Preheat oven to 180°C. In a bowl, toss potato slices with olive
   oil, rosemary, garlic and Parmesan. Place half of potatoes in
   a single layer on a baking tray and bake for 15 minutes or
   until golden. Set aside the uncooked potato slices.
2. Increase oven temperature to 200°C. Line two trays with
   baking paper.
3. Using a sharp knife, cut each pastry sheet into 30 rectangles
   measuring 5cm × 7cm. Place rectangles 2cm apart on lined
   baking trays.
4. Whisk together eggs and cream to form an egg wash. Brush
   over pastry. Score a line 3mm in from the edge of each
   galette to create a border.
5. Spread a thin layer of Rocket Pesto over each galette and top
   with a thin layer of uncooked potato slices. Cook in oven for
   20-25 minutes, until pastry and potato are well cooked.
6. Top each galette with fresh rocket, 5 slices of precooked
   potato and a piece of bocconcini. Drizzle with Balsamic
   Reduction and season with salt and pepper.

Chorizo Galettes

1. Prepare pastry for galettes by following steps 2-3 above.
2. Peel and chop 4 kumara into 1.5cm dice. Toss kumara in
   4 tablespoons olive oil, 4 tablespoons chopped rosemary, salt
   and pepper. Place on a baking tray and bake at 200°C for
   20 minutes.
3. Heat 2 tablespoons olive oil in a frying pan over high heat.
   Add 1 tablespoon paprika and 12 sliced chorizo sausages.
   Toss, then fry until golden and crispy.
4. Top each galette with 1 teaspoon Onion Jam (see page 186)
   and 3-4 kumara cubes. Bake at 200°C for 15 minutes or
   until golden. Sprinkle with blue cheese and bake a further
   5 minutes. Top with chorizo and chopped coriander leaves.
   Makes approximately 60.

little and friday.

Fig Galettes

Fig and blue cheese is a winning combination.

2 sheets Flaky Pastry (see page 182)

Topping
1 cup Onion Jam (see page 186)
25 fresh figs, cut into sixths
¼ cup manuka honey, warmed
1 cup crumbled blue cheese
12 slices prosciutto, torn

Egg Wash
2 eggs
2 tbsp cream

Makes approx. 60 petites galettes

1. Preheat oven to 200°C. Line two trays with baking paper.
2. Using a sharp knife, cut each pastry sheet into 30 rectangles measuring 5cm × 7cm. Place 2cm apart on lined baking trays.
3. Whisk together eggs and cream to form an egg wash. Brush over pastry. Score a line 3mm in from the edge of each galette to create a border.
4. Top each galette with 1 teaspoon Onion Jam and season with salt and pepper. Bake for 15 minutes or until golden.
5. Top each galette with 2–3 pieces of fig, drizzle with honey and sprinkle with blue cheese. Bake a further 5 minutes until cheese has melted. Top each galette with a piece of prosciutto, arranging it between cooked figs.

Chocolate Meringue Cakes

Rose Gray of the River Café in London was famous for her Chocolate Nemesis cake – a rich flourless chocolate cake. This is my version, which I have made as small cakes encased in Italian meringue to suit the white wedding buffet theme.

5 eggs

1½ cups caster sugar

65ml water

360g good-quality dark chocolate, chopped

225g unsalted butter

Meringue

50ml water

1 cup caster sugar

3 egg whites

Makes 12 small cakes

1. Preheat oven to 120°C. Grease and line a 12-hole 7cm-diameter patty tin with baking paper.
2. Using an electric mixer, whisk eggs with ½ cup sugar until mixture triples in volume – approximately 10 minutes. Set aside.
3. In a saucepan, combine remaining 1 cup sugar and water. Boil for 2 minutes. Cool.
4. In a glass bowl over a pot of simmering water, combine chocolate and butter. Stir until melted. Slowly drizzle sugar syrup into melted chocolate, stirring constantly. Allow to cool for 5 minutes.
5. Using a large metal spoon, fold chocolate mixture through beaten eggs until completely combined.
6. Pour batter into prepared patty tin. Tap the tin to release air bubbles. Place in a baking tray and carefully pour boiling water to halfway up the sides of the patty tin. Bake for 1 hour, or until a thin crust forms on top.
7. Remove from oven and leave to cool, then refrigerate for 2 hours before inverting tin onto a tray to remove cakes. Cakes will be very soft.
8. To make meringue, combine water and sugar in a saucepan over medium heat. Using a wet pastry brush, remove loose sugar crystals from sides of pan. Bring to the boil, then reduce heat and cook without stirring until mixture reaches 114°C on a candy thermometer.
9. Meanwhile, using an electric mixer, whisk egg whites until soft peaks form.
10. Continue cooking sugar syrup until mixture reaches 116°C on a candy thermometer. Place saucepan in cold water for a few seconds to prevent further cooking.
11. Slowly drizzle syrup into beaten egg whites. Do not do this

little and friday.

too quickly, or the egg whites will collapse. Beat on high speed until the mixture cools down (7–10 minutes).

12. Using a palette knife, spread a thick coating of meringue over each chocolate cake and place in refrigerator for at least 30 minutes. The tips of the meringue can be lightly caramelised with a cook's blowtorch.

Kitchen Notes
The cakes can be cooked up to two days in advance. Italian meringue, made with hot sugar syrup which cooks the egg whites, has a firm, glossy set and requires no further baking.

Pistachio Nougat

Soft nougat is great to add to ice cream and mousse.

1 packet edible rice paper
3 cups caster sugar
½ cup manuka honey
½ cup liquid glucose
3 egg whites
2 cups pistachios
⅓ cup cornflour
½ cup icing sugar
extra icing sugar, for dusting

Makes approx. 36 pieces

1. Line a 28cm × 18cm sponge roll tin with edible rice paper.
2. In a heavy-based saucepan, combine sugar, honey and glucose and stir with a wooden spoon over medium heat until sugar dissolves, approximately 10 minutes. Brush down sides of saucepan with a wet pastry brush to prevent sugar crystallising. Increase heat and bring to the boil. Reduce heat and boil without stirring until mixture reaches 120°C on a candy thermometer.
3. Meanwhile, using an electric mixer, whisk egg whites until stiff peaks form.
4. Continue cooking sugar syrup until mixture reaches 140°C on a candy thermometer. Place saucepan in cold water for a minute to stop mixture cooking.
5. With electric mixer on medium speed, slowly drizzle sugar mixture into whisked egg whites and beat for 3–5 minutes or until mixture is glossy. Using a large metal spoon, fold pistachios through mixture.
6. In a separate bowl, combine cornflour and icing sugar.
7. Pour nougat mixture onto a clean surface and dust in icing sugar mixture. Press into prepared tray, stretching to fit. You will need to work swiftly as the nougat becomes firm quickly.
8. Cover nougat with remaining rice paper and leave to set for 6 hours in a cool, dry place. Once set, use a serrated knife to cut into bars measuring approximately 7cm × 2cm and dust with icing sugar.

Kitchen Notes
Edible rice paper is available from specialty food stores.

Nougat may be stored in an airtight container in a cool place for up to two weeks. If the edges become moist, just cut them off; the centre will still be firm.

Lime Meringue Tartlets

The lime filling for these Italian meringue-topped tartlets
must be made a day ahead, but will keep for up to a week
in the refrigerator in an airtight container.

1 double recipe Sweet Pastry
(see page 182)

Filling
7 eggs
1½ cups caster sugar
220ml cream
zest and juice of 8 limes

Meringue
100ml water
1¾ cups caster sugar
6 egg whites

Makes 24 tartlets

1. To prepare filling, in a large bowl combine eggs, sugar and cream and stir with a whisk until sugar has dissolved. Don't beat the mixture, as you don't want it to become aerated. Add lime zest and juice and stir for 2 minutes. Cover and refrigerate overnight.

2. Preheat oven to 180°C. Grease and line two 12-hole 7cm-diameter patty tins with baking paper (see Helpful Hints, page 7).

3. Roll out pastry to 3mm thick. Using a 10cm-diameter cookie cutter, cut out 24 circles. Roll very lightly a second time, being careful not to roll too thin.

4. Line patty tins with pastry and rest pastry in refrigerator for 20 minutes. Use a sharp knife to trim off any overhanging pastry.

5. Line pastry with paper patty cases and fill with uncooked rice or dried beans. Blind bake for 15 minutes or until golden. Cool before removing paper cases and rice or beans.

6. Reduce oven temperature to 150°C and bake pastry cases for another 10 minutes. Cool. Reduce oven temperature to 100°C.

7. Stir lime filling for a minute to combine. Strain through a fine sieve into a large jug and skim any froth from the top. Fill baked pastry cases with lime filling. Bake for 30 minutes or until set – the filling should wobble slightly when the tray is moved. Cool before carefully removing from tins.

8. To make meringue, combine water and sugar in a saucepan over medium heat. Using a wet pastry brush, remove loose sugar crystals from sides of pan. Bring to the boil, then reduce heat and cook without stirring until mixture reaches 114°C on a candy thermometer.

9. Meanwhile, using an electric mixer, whisk egg whites until soft peaks form.

10. Continue cooking sugar syrup until mixture reaches 116°C.

little and friday.

Place saucepan in cold water for a few seconds to prevent further cooking.

11. Slowly drizzle syrup into beaten egg whites. Do not do this too quickly or the egg whites will collapse. Beat on high speed until the mixture cools (7–10 minutes).

12. Top each tart with a spoonful of meringue, which can be lightly caramelised with a cook's blowtorch, if desired (see Kitchen Notes, page 101).

Kaffir Lime and Coconut Brûlées

Kaffir lime and coconut give the classic brûlée a tropical
tang. These are best made two days ahead.

2½ cups cream
1 cup coconut cream
½ cinnamon quill
½ vanilla bean
6 fresh Kaffir lime leaves
10 egg yolks
½ cup caster sugar, plus extra
for topping

Makes 6

1. In a saucepan, combine cream, coconut cream, cinnamon,
   vanilla and Kaffir lime leaves and bring to a simmer. Remove
   from heat, pour into an airtight container and refrigerate
   overnight.
2. Preheat oven to 120°C.
3. Place cream mixture into a saucepan and bring to a boil.
   Remove from heat immediately and cool. Strain through a
   sieve and discard the spices and leaves.
4. Using an electric mixer, whisk egg yolks and sugar until pale
   and creamy. Add a quarter of the cream to egg mixture and
   whisk to combine. Pour remaining cream into egg mixture
   and whisk to combine.
5. Divide mixture among 6 heatproof individual serving dishes
   and place in a roasting pan. Pour hot water into pan to reach
   halfway up the sides of the dishes. Cook in centre of oven for
   30–35 minutes or until just set.
6. Remove brûlée dishes from pan and cool for 30–35 minutes
   before placing in refrigerator overnight.
7. To serve, sprinkle with extra caster sugar and caramelise
   using a cook's blowtorch, or place under a hot grill for
   5 minutes until caramelised.

White Chocolate and Berry Mousse

This mousse is delicious on its own, but I amped it up a little
with the addition of nougat.

4 egg yolks

2 tbsp caster sugar

2½ cups cream

400g white chocolate, chopped

24 fresh blackberries or
raspberries

Pistachio Nougat, chopped, to
garnish (see page 102)

8 Meringue Kisses, to serve (see
page 110)

Serves 8

1. Place egg yolks and sugar in a bowl and whisk until pale.
2. Place ½ cup cream in a saucepan over low heat and bring to a
   simmer. Slowly add cream to whisked eggs. Return mixture
   to saucepan and stir over low heat until the mixture coats
   the back of a wooden spoon. Pour through a sieve into a bowl
   and set aside.
3. Meanwhile, melt chocolate in a glass bowl over a saucepan of
   simmering water, making sure the water does not touch the
   base of the bowl. When the chocolate and the cream mixture
   are a similar temperature, add the chocolate to the cream
   mixture and mix until combined.
4. In another bowl, whip remaining 2 cups cream until almost
   stiff peaks. Fold half the whipped cream into the chocolate
   mixture, being careful not to overmix. Fold in remaining
   cream.
5. Spoon into 8 cups or serving glasses and refrigerate until set,
   approximately 1 hour. When ready to serve, garnish with
   blackberries or raspberries, chopped nougat and a Meringue
   Kiss (Meringue Kiss-topped mousse pictured on page 92).

Kitchen Notes
Use extra-tart blackberries to cut through the sweetness of
the mousse.

Meringue Kisses

These are an easy dessert that can be made up to a week ahead. Sandwich together with icing, cream or ganache for a more flavoured result.

6 egg whites
1 cup caster sugar
1 cup icing sugar

Makes 80–100

1. Preheat oven to 80°C. Line two trays with baking paper.
2. Using an electric mixer, whisk egg whites until soft peaks form. With mixer on medium speed, slowly add caster sugar a tablespoon at a time. Once caster sugar is absorbed into the meringue, beat for a further 10 minutes until glossy.
3. Sift icing sugar into meringue. Using a large metal spoon, fold it through the meringue, being careful not to deflate the mixture.
4. Place meringue in a piping bag fitted with a medium star nozzle and pipe meringue in small kisses onto baking trays.
5. Bake for 1½ hours or until meringues are dry and lift easily off the tray.

Kitchen Notes
Store Meringue Kisses in an airtight container for up to one week.

Cardamom and White Chocolate Wedding Cake

This impressive layered cake forms the bottom tier of a two-tier
wedding cake. The top tier and instructions for assembly
are over the page.

5 eggs

2½ cups caster sugar

300ml canola oil

1½ cups good-quality white
chocolate, chopped

1 tsp vanilla extract or essence

seeds of 10 green cardamom
pods, crushed in a mortar
and pestle

2¼ cups plain flour

2 tsp baking powder

200ml milk

White Chocolate Ganache

1 cup cream

400g good-quality white
chocolate, grated

Makes one 20cm triple-layer cake

1. Preheat oven to 150°C. Grease three 20cm round cake tins
   and line the bottoms and sides with baking paper.
2. Using an electric mixer, whisk eggs and sugar at high speed
   until mixture triples in volume. With mixer on low speed,
   slowly drizzle in oil.
3. Melt chocolate in a glass bowl over a saucepan of simmering
   water.
4. Add vanilla, crushed cardamom seeds and melted chocolate
   to egg mixture and mix to combine.
5. Sift flour and baking powder into a bowl. Using a large metal
   spoon, fold a third of the dry ingredients into chocolate
   mixture. When almost combined, add a third of the milk.
   Continue until all combined.
6. Pour mixture evenly into prepared tins. Bake in centre of
   oven for 35–40 minutes or until a skewer comes out clean.
   Cool in tins before assembling.
7. To make White Chocolate Ganache, in a saucepan heat cream
   until just below boiling. Place chocolate in a bowl and pour
   hot cream over. Stir vigorously to combine. Once smooth,
   place in a dry place out of the sun to set.
8. To assemble, turn out cakes and, using a large serrated knife,
   slice off the domed tops to create a flat surface. Place one
   cake onto a 20cm-diameter cardboard disc. Spread with half
   the White Chocolate Ganache. Top with a second layer of
   cake and the remaining ganache. Place the final layer of cake
   on top and refrigerate until ready to ice with Buttercream
   Icing (see page 115).

Kitchen Notes

Ganache is best made a day ahead.

little and friday.

Passionfruit and Yoghurt Wedding Cake

This forms the top tier of the wedding cake pictured on page 113, but is a delicious cake in its own right.

pulp of 10 passionfruit
300g unsalted butter
2½ cups caster sugar
1 tbsp lemon zest
6 eggs
3 cups plain flour
2½ tsp baking powder
¾ cup plain yoghurt

Passionfruit Filling
2 cups mascarpone
pulp of 10 passionfruit

Makes one 15cm triple-layer cake

1. Preheat oven to 150°C. Grease three 15cm round cake tins and line the bottoms and sides with baking paper.
2. Place passionfruit pulp in a sieve over a bowl and use a spoon to extract juice. Discard seeds and set juice aside.
3. Using an electric mixer, on medium speed beat butter, sugar and lemon zest until pale and fluffy. Add eggs one at a time, mixing well after each addition. Regularly scrape down sides of bowl with a spatula.
4. Sift flour and baking powder over butter mixture and fold through using a large metal spoon. Be careful not to overmix. Fold through reserved passionfruit juice and yoghurt.
5. Pour mixture evenly into prepared tins. Bake in centre of oven for 35–40 minutes, or until a skewer comes out clean. Cool in tins before assembling.
6. To make filling, combine mascarpone and passionfruit pulp.
7. To assemble, turn out cakes and, using a large serrated knife, slice off the domed tops to create a flat surface. Place one cake onto a 15cm-diameter cardboard disc. Spread with half the filling. Top with a second layer of cake and the remaining filling. Place the final layer of cake on top and refrigerate until ready to ice with Buttercream Icing.

Sugar Roses
Remove centres from 10–12 roses. Lightly whisk 3 egg whites and, using a 1cm paintbrush, cover outer petals on both sides with egg white. Sprinkle with caster sugar to coat. Hang roses upside down to dry for 1–2 days. Drying time will depend on the humidity. Once dry, ease out petals to get a full look.

To Assemble Wedding Cake

Putting it all together!

Buttercream Icing
1 cup caster sugar
¼ cup water
5 egg whites
450g unsalted butter

1. Combine sugar and water in a heavy-based saucepan over medium heat. Stir with a wooden spoon until the sugar dissolves, approximately 10 minutes. Using a wet pastry brush to remove sugar crystals from sides of pan.
2. Increase heat to high and bring syrup to the boil. Reduce heat and continue to boil without stirring until mixture reaches 116°C on a candy thermometer.
3. Using an electric mixer, whisk egg whites until soft peaks form.
4. Continue cooking syrup until mixture reaches 118°C on a candy thermometer. Remove from heat and place saucepan in cold water for a minute to stop syrup cooking.
5. With electric mixer on medium speed, slowly drizzle syrup into egg whites. Once combined, turn mixer to high and whisk for 6–10 minutes until mixture cools. Add butter a little at a time and beat until well combined. Place icing in refrigerator for 2 hours until firm.
6. Thread four bamboo skewers into each cake from the top to secure the layers. Cut off protruding ends of skewers.
7. Using a large serrated knife, trim sides of cakes to form a clean edge.
8. Using a palette knife, spread a thin layer of Buttercream Icing over each cake. This is called a scratch coat, to stop crumbs from coming away. Refrigerate for 30 minutes.
9. Spread a thicker layer of icing over each cake and, using a plastic scraper (such as a strip cut from an ice-cream container), smooth the icing. Refrigerate for a further 30 minutes.
10. Using two knives, lift the smaller cake onto the top of the larger cake, making sure it is perfectly centred. Arrange Sugar Roses (see opposite) on the top cake and place 3 Sugar Roses on the bottom layer and at the base of the cake. (Allow the cake to come to room temperature, approximately 3 hours, before serving.)

HIGH TEA

There aren't many occasions these days to dress up
for and play ladies. Sometimes you have to create
one. Find a beautiful outdoor location and invite the
girls for delicate bites, dainty sweets and a good
cup of tea served off pretty china.

Club Sandwiches

Strawberry Cream Puffs

Éclairs

Green Tea Sponge Roll

Chocolate Macaroons

Rose Cupcakes

Chocolate Marshmallow Puffs

Club Sandwiches

A good club sandwich is a must for any high tea.

1 red capsicum
2 hardboiled eggs
¼ cup Aïoli (see page 184)
1 tsp chopped chives
salt and freshly ground pepper
2 avocados
½ lemon
softened butter, for spreading
6 slices white sandwich bread
8 toothpicks
8 pitted green olives

Makes 8 square club sandwiches

Egg Club Sandwiches

1. Preheat oven to 180°C. Cut capsicum in half, deseed, and roast for 10 minutes. Remove from oven and leave to cool.
2. In a bowl, mash together hardboiled eggs, Aïoli and chives. Season with salt and pepper.
3. Peel and dice avocados and put in a bowl. Squeeze lemon juice over. Add diced roast capsicum and stir gently to combine.
4. Butter each slice of bread. Spread a thick layer of egg mixture over two slices. Place another layer of bread on top, and spread with a thick layer of avocado mixture. Top with a final layer of bread butter-side down.
5. Wrap sandwiches securely in baking paper and place a heavy book on top to gently flatten them. Refrigerate for at least 30 minutes or until ready to serve.
6. Remove sandwiches from refrigerator. Unwrap and, using a good bread knife, cut off crusts and cut each sandwich into four. Pierce each sandwich with a toothpick to hold it together, and thread an olive onto each toothpick.

Corned Beef Club Sandwiches

Butter 6 slices white sandwich bread. Place 2 slices English Cheddar and 20 thin slices cucumber on two of the slices of bread. Season with salt and pepper. Top each with another slice of bread. Lay two 8mm-thick slices corned beef on top of bread and spread with tomato relish. Top with remaining bread slices. Continue as in steps 5–6 above, and secure with lengths of baking paper and ribbon.

Kitchen Notes

To prevent sandwiches from drying out, cover with a damp tea towel until ready to serve.

little and friday.

Strawberry Cream Puffs

This Choux Pastry recipe can also be used to make Éclairs
(see page 122).

Choux Pastry

180ml milk

180ml water

150g unsalted butter

¼ tsp salt

¼ tsp caster sugar

1¾ cups flour

8 eggs, beaten

Strawberry Cream Puffs

1 recipe Choux Pastry (see above)

1 recipe Crème Pâtissière (see page 188)

Crème Chantilly

250ml cream

¼ cup icing sugar, sifted

1 tsp vanilla extract

Strawberry Icing

1 cup icing sugar, sifted

2 fresh strawberries

Makes approx. 40 cream puffs (or 25 small éclairs)

1. Preheat oven to 200°C. Line two trays with baking paper.
2. Place milk, water, butter, salt and sugar in a saucepan over medium heat. Stirring occasionally, bring to just before the boil.
3. Remove from heat and add flour. Beat vigorously with a wooden spoon to a smooth ball of paste that leaves sides of saucepan clean. Keep stirring to cool slightly.
4. Add eggs to the cooled mixture a little at a time, thoroughly beating in each addition before adding the next.
5. Beat to a smooth glossy paste (approximately 5 minutes).
6. Spoon mixture into a piping bag with a star nozzle, and pipe onto trays. For cream puffs, pipe 4cm-diameter spirals, with the centre coming to a peak. For éclairs, pipe 8cm x 2cm tube shapes. Place 2cm apart, as they will spread. Alternatively, use teaspoons to form cream puffs and éclairs.
7. Place in top of oven and bake for 20–30 minutes. Reduce oven temperature to 160°C and bake for a further 15 minutes. Do not open the oven door during baking, as cases will deflate. Cool before filling.

Strawberry Cream Puffs

1. Slice the cooled choux pastry puffs in half horizontally.
2. Spoon Crème Pâtissière into a piping bag and fill the cavities of both top and bottom halves.
3. Spoon Crème Chantilly (see below) into a piping bag fitted with a star nozzle and pipe a spiral of cream onto the filled base of the cream puff, then sandwich with the top half.
4. To make Strawberry Icing, blitz icing sugar and strawberries in a food processor to a smooth, runny consistency.

Crème Chantilly

Beat cream until stiff. Slowly add icing sugar and vanilla. Beat for 1 minute. Store covered in refrigerator for up to three days.

little and friday.

Éclairs

Light and delicate, these are a perfect tea-time treat.
The éclairs can be made a day ahead and assembled
just before serving.

1 recipe Choux Pastry (see
page 120)
1 recipe Crème Pâtissière (see
page 188)
Pink Fondant (see below)
sugar flowers, for decoration
(see page 114)

Pink Fondant
1 cup caster sugar
100ml water
pink food colouring

Makes 25 small éclairs

1. Make Choux Pastry by following recipe on page 120.
2. To fill éclairs, using a skewer poke a hole in one end of the éclair cases to create a central cavity.
3. Using a piping bag, pipe Crème Pâtissière into each cavity until the éclair slightly expands.
4. Ice éclairs with soft Pink Fondant and decorate with sugar flowers (see page 114).

Pink Fondant

1. Combine sugar and water in a heavy-based saucepan and place over a medium heat. Brush down sides of saucepan with a wet pastry brush to prevent sugar crystallising, and cook until the temperature reaches 114°C on a candy thermometer. Stand saucepan in cold water and cool mixture until it reaches 75°C on the candy thermometer.
2. Pour syrup into the bowl of an electric mixer and beat for 5 minutes until thick. Turn mixture out onto a bench dusted with cornflour and lightly knead to form a ball. Wrap in cling film and store in the refrigerator. It will keep for up to six months.
3. To ice éclairs, heat fondant in a microwave or in a saucepan over a low heat until it becomes runny. Add a few drops of pink food colouring and stir to combine. Spread over the tops of the éclairs.

Green Tea Sponge Roll

My Japanese pastry chef Kohei created this version of a
classic sponge roll.

5 eggs, separated, plus 1 extra
egg white
¾ cup caster sugar
½ cup flour, sifted
2 tsp fine green tea powder
25g unsalted butter, melted
25ml milk

Crème Chantilly
200ml cream
2 tbsp icing sugar, sifted
1 tsp Cointreau

extra icing sugar and green tea
powder, to decorate

Makes one 35cm roll

1. Preheat oven to 180°C. Line a 35cm × 25cm sponge roll tin
   with baking paper.
2. Using an electric mixer, whisk 5 egg yolks and ¼ cup caster
   sugar until the mixture is thick enough to produce ribbons
   when the whisk is lifted out of the mixture. Remove mixture
   to another bowl.
3. In the clean and dry mixer bowl, whisk all 6 egg whites until
   soft peaks form.
4. With the mixer on medium speed, add remaining ½ cup sugar
   gradually, a spoonful at a time, and beat until stiff peaks form.
5. Using a metal spoon, fold egg white mixture into egg yolk
   mixture. Gently fold in sifted flour and green tea powder.
   Lastly, fold in melted butter and milk. Be careful not to
   overmix or the sponge mixture will lose air.
6. Pour mixture into prepared tin, place in centre of oven and
   lower oven temperature to 120°C. Bake for 20 minutes
   (refrain from opening the door during this time), or until top
   springs back when lightly touched.
7. Turn the sponge out onto a tea towel and leave to cool for
   2 minutes. Then, with the long side facing you, use the tea
   towel to roll it up into a tight log. Leave to cool completely,
   wrapped in the tea towel.
8. While the sponge is cooling, make the Crème Chantilly. Beat
   cream until stiff peaks form. Add icing sugar and Cointreau
   and gently mix.
9. To assemble the sponge roll, unroll the tea towel and spoon
   the Crème Chantilly onto the sponge, spreading to 1cm thick
   all over. Reroll the sponge, cover with a damp tea towel and
   refrigerate for at least 1 hour before cutting. Sift icing sugar
   and extra green tea powder over to serve.

Kitchen Notes
For green tea powder, use the contents of a green tea bag.

little and friday.

Chocolate Macaroons

Only make macaroons in dry weather, when they will form a crust.

1 cup icing sugar
1 cup ground almonds
5 tbsp good-quality cocoa
3 egg whites
⅓ cup caster sugar
50ml water
1 cup Chocolate Ganache
(see page 187)

Raspberry Cream
125g raspberries
⅔ cup caster sugar
100ml cream
100g mascarpone
¼ cup icing sugar, sifted
handful of raspberries

Makes approx. 24

1. Line a tray with baking paper.
2. Place icing sugar, ground almonds and cocoa in a food processor and blitz until well combined. Sift three times into a bowl and set aside. Add 2 egg whites and mix to a paste.
3. Place caster sugar in a saucepan over medium heat. Add water and stir to form a paste. Bring to the boil.
4. Meanwhile, whisk remaining egg white to soft peaks. Heat sugar mixture to 118°C on a candy thermometer. Remove from heat and slowly add to beaten egg white. Beat for 7 minutes until mixture cools. Using a large metal spoon, fold almond mixture into egg white mixture in batches.
5. Spoon macaroon mixture into a piping bag fitted with a 1cm nozzle. Pipe 3cm-diameter blobs of mixture onto prepared tray, leaving a 1cm gap between each macaroon. Leave to stand for 1–2 hours to form a crust.
6. Preheat oven to 150°C. Bake macaroons in the middle of the preheated oven for 15 minutes until risen.
7. To assemble macaroons, pipe or spread a dollop of Chocolate Ganache on half the macaroons and top with the remaining macaroons to form a sandwich. Refrigerate until required.

Macaroons with Raspberry Cream
Omit cocoa and add ½ teaspoon freeze-dried raspberry powder (see page 40) to the almond-icing sugar mixture when folding it into the whisked egg whites. Sandwich the macaroons with Raspberry Cream. (See photograph page 116.)

Raspberry Cream
1. Place raspberries and sugar in a saucepan over medium heat and bring to the boil. Reduce heat and simmer for 2 minutes. Cool.
2. Whisk cream into soft peaks. Add mascarpone and beat for 1 minute. On low speed, add icing sugar. Stir through raspberries.

little and friday.

Rose Cupcakes

These cupcakes are delicious with just a simple little violet
on top. I went all out and dressed them up with sugar flowers,
which are available from a cake decorating supplier.

125g unsalted butter
1 cup caster sugar
3 eggs
1½ cups flour
1 tsp baking powder
½ cup milk, at room
temperature
28 sugar flowers, to decorate

Rose Icing

1 cup icing sugar
½ tsp rosewater
5 tbsp hot water

Makes 24 petite cupcakes

1. Preheat oven to 160°C. Grease two 12-hole small muffin
   trays. Cut strips of baking paper approximately 4cm × 10cm,
   and use these to line sides of each tin so they extend 1cm
   above the rims. Place cupcake cases into lined tins.
2. Using an electric mixer, beat butter and sugar until pale
   and fluffy.
3. Add eggs one at a time, mixing well after each addition.
   Scrape down sides of bowl after each addition.
4. Sift flour and baking powder into a bowl. Using a large spoon,
   fold flour mixture and milk alternately into creamed mixture
   until combined. Use a teaspoon to fill cupcake cases to the top.
5. Bake in centre of oven for 15 minutes, or until cupcake
   tops spring back when lightly touched. Cool in tins before
   turning out.
6. To make Rose Icing, sift icing sugar into a bowl, stir in
   rosewater and hot water, and mix to spreadable consistency.
7. Ice cupcakes with Rose Icing and decorate with a sugar
   flower.

Kitchen Notes
Having the milk at room temperature prevents the mixture from
splitting.

Sugar flowers are available from specialty cake decorating stores, or
make your own using edible flowers, such as pansies or violets, and
see page 114 for instructions.

little and friday.

Chocolate Marshmallow Puffs

This recipe requires a bit of preparation. The cookie dough needs to rest for at least an hour and you need to allow time for the marshmallow and chocolate to set, but these popular tea-time treats are worth the extra effort.

3 cups flour
½ cup caster sugar
½ tsp salt
¾ tsp baking powder
½ tsp baking soda
½ tsp cinnamon
170g unsalted butter
3 eggs

Marshmallow

6 sheets gelatine, or 1 tbsp powdered gelatine
2 tbsp cold water
¼ cup water
¼ cup glucose syrup
¾ cup caster sugar
2 egg whites
seeds from 1 vanilla bean

Chocolate Glaze

340g good-quality dark chocolate, chopped
60g cocoa butter

Makes approx. 24

1. To make the biscuit bases, mix dry ingredients on low speed using an electric mixer. Add butter and mix to fine crumbs.
2. Add eggs one at a time, mixing well after each addition.
3. Using your hands, form dough into a ball, wrap in cling film and refrigerate for at least an hour or overnight. The dough will keep in the refrigerator for up to one week.
4. When ready to cook the biscuits, preheat oven to 180°C. Line two baking trays with baking paper.
5. On a well-floured surface, roll out dough to 5mm thick. Use a 3cm-diameter cookie cutter to cut out 24 biscuits. Transfer to prepared baking trays and bake for 10 minutes. Cool biscuits on a rack while you make the marshmallow.
6. If using gelatine sheets, cover with 2 tablespoons cold water and soak for 5 minutes.
7. In a saucepan, combine ¼ cup water, glucose syrup and sugar. Bring to the boil, and boil until mixture reaches 110°C on a candy thermometer.
8. Remove gelatine sheets from water and squeeze out excess water using a clean tea towel. Remove syrup from heat and add the gelatine sheets or powder, stirring to combine.
9. Using an electric mixer, whisk egg whites until soft peaks form. On medium speed, slowly drizzle the syrup into the egg whites. Don't add it too fast or the egg whites will collapse. Add vanilla seeds and continue whisking until stiff peaks form (approximately 10 minutes). Transfer mixture to a piping bag.
10. Pipe a kiss of marshmallow onto each cookie. Leave to set at room temperature for 2 hours.
11. When ready to glaze, melt chocolate and cocoa butter in a glass bowl over a saucepan of simmering water. Stir until smooth.
12. Line a tray with baking paper. Gently dunk biscuits into warm chocolate glaze. Lift out with a fork, letting excess

little and friday.

chocolate drip back into the bowl. Place on tray and leave to set at room temperature (approximately 2 hours). Store in an airtight container for up to one week.

Kitchen Notes
Cocoa butter is available from specialty food stores. Alternatively, dip in melted chocolate.

High Tea

MOTHER'S DAY

This Mother's Day get-together features food my
mother made for me in the 1970s and 1980s, when
I was the same age as my daughter Holly is now.
I would have loved for Mum to be present to share our
day, but due to her health it wasn't possible. Instead,
she is included through the recipes and photographs
of her as a little girl. As we went to print we welcomed
a new generation to our family – another sassy
Little and Friday girl, Willow Plum.

Pastizzi

Pumpkin and Goat's Cheese Tart

Mushroom Quiche

Peanut Monkeys

Sesame Fingers

Apple and Ricotta Shortcakes

Portuguese Custard Tarts

Blood Orange Baby Cakes

Pastizzi

I lived in Sydney in the 1980s and would queue up every Sunday
morning to buy pastizzi from a wee shop in Crown Street. The baker
was around eighty years old and made the best pastizzi outside of
Malta. This recipe is the closest I've come to re-creating it.

1 recipe Flaky Pastry (see
page 182)
4 cups baby spinach
¼ cup water
300g ricotta
½ cup grated tasty cheese
2 eggs
salt and freshly ground pepper

Egg Wash
2 eggs
2 tbsp cream

Makes 12–14

1. Preheat oven to 200°C. Line two trays with baking paper.
2. On a floured bench, roll out pastry to 3mm thick. Using a
   10cm-diameter cookie cutter, cut out 12 circles. Place pastry
   circles 3cm apart on prepared trays and refrigerate for
   15 minutes.
3. Wash spinach and place in a saucepan with water over
   medium heat. Cook until just wilted. Cool and squeeze out
   excess moisture.
4. In a bowl, combine spinach, ricotta, grated cheese, eggs
   and salt and pepper, and mix well. Place a tablespoonful of
   spinach mixture on the centre of each pastry circle.
5. Make egg wash by whisking together eggs and cream in a
   small bowl. Brush the edges of the pastry with egg wash and
   bring together to form a boat shape. Pinch the ends of the
   pastry together to seal, leaving an opening in the top so the
   spinach can be seen. Brush pastry with extra egg wash.
6. Bake in oven for 30 minutes or until golden. Serve hot.

Pumpkin and Goat's Cheese Tart

This makes a nice vegetarian option if you omit the pancetta.

1 recipe Paprika & Gruyère Pastry (see below)

4 cups pumpkin, cut into 2cm dice

handful of fresh marjoram leaves

1 nutmeg, grated

4 tbsp extra virgin olive oil

salt and freshly ground pepper

¾ cup grated Parmesan

2 cups baby spinach

1½ cups crumbled goat's cheese

6 slices pancetta, chopped

12 eggs

⅓ cup cream

Paprika & Gruyère Pastry

75g unsalted butter

1¼ cups flour

½ tsp paprika

½ tsp mustard powder

½ cup grated Gruyère

salt and freshly ground pepper

1 egg yolk

2 tbsp iced water

Makes one 28cm round tart

1. Preheat oven to 180°C. Grease a 28cm round loose-bottom tart tin.
2. On a floured bench, roll out pastry to 3mm thick. Line base and sides of prepared tin, trimming edges. Refrigerate for at least 30 minutes.
3. Meanwhile, place pumpkin on a lined baking tray. Add marjoram, grated nutmeg, olive oil and salt and pepper, and toss to coat pumpkin. Roast in oven for 20 minutes. Cool.
4. Sprinkle pastry case with Parmesan. Top with spinach and season with salt and pepper.
5. Arrange cooled pumpkin over spinach and sprinkle with goat's cheese and pancetta.
6. In a large jug, whisk eggs and cream to combine and pour into filled pastry case to 2mm below the rim. Season with salt and pepper.
7. Bake in centre of oven for 50 minutes, until filling is set. Check by pressing gently on top of the tart; if no liquid seeps out, it is ready.

Paprika & Gruyère Pastry

1. In a bowl, rub butter into flour until mixture resembles fine breadcrumbs.
2. In a separate bowl, mix together paprika, mustard powder, Gruyère and salt and pepper. Mix in egg yolk and water.
3. Add cheese mixture to flour mixture and lightly knead together to form a soft dough.
4. Wrap dough in cling film and rest in the refrigerator for at least 30 minutes before using.

Mushroom Quiche

This may seem like a lot of butter to cook the mushrooms in, but they will soak it all up and have a beautiful flavour as a result.

1 recipe Paprika & Gruyère
Pastry (see page 136)
250g unsalted butter
8 cloves garlic, crushed
1kg button mushrooms, sliced
handful of fresh thyme leaves
salt and freshly ground pepper
12 eggs
⅓ cup cream
¾ cup grated Parmesan
1½ cups chopped bacon
Baked Button Mushrooms, to
garnish (see below)

Baked Button Mushrooms
12 button mushrooms
rind and juice of 2 lemons
salt and freshly ground pepper
several sprigs of thyme

Makes one 28cm round quiche

1. Grease a 28cm round loose-bottom tart tin.
2. On a floured bench, roll out pastry to 3mm thick. Line base and sides of prepared tin with pastry, trimming edges. Leave to rest in refrigerator for at least 30 minutes.
3. Melt butter in a frying pan over medium heat and cook garlic for 1 minute. Add mushrooms and cook until mushrooms soften. Add thyme leaves and season with salt and pepper. Set aside to cool.
4. Preheat oven to 180°C. Place lined tart tin on a baking tray.
5. Sprinkle unbaked pastry case with Parmesan. Spoon cooked mushrooms into pastry case and scatter bacon over.
6. In a large jug, whisk eggs and cream to combine and pour into filled pastry case to 2mm below the rim. Season with salt and pepper.
7. Bake in centre of oven for 50 minutes, until filling is set. Check by pressing gently on top of quiche; if no liquid seeps out, it is ready. Serve with Baked Button Mushrooms.

Baked Button Mushrooms
Preheat oven to 230°C. Place button mushrooms (stalks up) on a baking tray. Peel rind from lemons using a vegetable peeler and place on top of mushrooms. Squeeze the lemon juice over. Season with salt and pepper and sprinkle thyme sprigs over. Cover with foil and bake for 10 minutes. Serve cooked mushrooms with quiche and garnish with more thyme.

Peanut Monkeys

This is our decadent version of the classic peanut brownie.

180g good-quality dark chocolate, chopped
125g unsalted butter
1 cup caster sugar
1 egg
1½ cups flour
1 tsp baking powder
2 tbsp good-quality cocoa
1 cup roasted salted peanuts
200g good-quality dark chocolate, for dipping (optional)

Makes approx. 25

1. Line two baking trays with baking paper.
2. Melt first measure of chocolate in a double boiler or in a bowl over a saucepan of simmering water. Cool.
3. Using an electric mixer, beat butter and sugar until pale and fluffy. Add egg and mix to combine.
4. Add melted chocolate to creamed mixture and stir to combine.
5. Sift flour, baking powder and cocoa into a separate bowl. Using a large metal spoon, fold dry ingredients into chocolate mixture. Stir in roasted peanuts until well combined.
6. Roll mixture into walnut-sized balls. Place 2cm apart on prepared trays, slightly flatten with a fork, and refrigerate for 1 hour.
7. Preheat oven to 180°C. Bake biscuits in oven for 15 minutes.
8. If desired, melt second measure of chocolate and coat one half of each biscuit in melted chocolate.

Sesame Fingers

This recipe was given to my mother by a dear friend called Richie,
so as a child I always called this 'Richie's Stuff'.

2 cups shredded coconut
2 cups flour
2 cups brown sugar
4 cups jumbo rolled oats
pinch of salt
3 tsp fennel seeds
6 tbsp sesame seeds
360g unsalted butter, melted

Makes approx. 24 slices

1. Preheat oven to 180°C. Grease and line a 25cm square tin with baking paper.
2. Place all ingredients except butter in a large bowl. Pour melted butter over, and mix to combine.
3. Press mixture firmly into prepared tin. Bake for 25 minutes until pale golden.
4. Cool, then cut into fingers before turning out.

little and friday.

Apple and Ricotta Shortcakes

Plums, apricots or figs can be used in place of apples in these cakes.

90g unsalted butter

1 cup caster sugar

zest of 1 lemon

3 eggs

1 cup grated apple

⅔ cup flour

1 tsp baking powder

1 cup ground almonds

50ml milk

350g ricotta

1 egg yolk

2 tbsp manuka honey

2 tbsp walnut paste

2 Granny Smith apples, cored and sliced

Crumble

½ cup flour

pinch of salt

40g cold unsalted butter, diced

3 tsp white sugar

3 tsp brown sugar

¼ cup walnuts

1 tsp cinnamon

To garnish

250g mascarpone

Dried Apple Slices (see right)

Makes 12 small cakes

1. Preheat oven to 180°C. Grease and line 12 dariole moulds or a 12-hole muffin tray with baking paper cut to extend 1cm above the rims.
2. Using an electric mixer, beat butter, ¾ cup sugar and lemon zest until pale and creamy. Add whole eggs one at a time, mixing well after each addition. Add grated apple and mix to combine.
3. Sift flour and baking powder into a separate bowl. Add ground almonds and stir to combine. Using a large metal spoon, fold a third of the flour mixture into the creamed mixture, followed by a third of the milk. Continue until all combined.
4. Spread mixture into prepared tins.
5. Place ricotta, egg yolk and remaining ¼ cup caster sugar in a food processor and blitz to combine. Add honey and walnut paste and blitz for a further minute.
6. Spoon ricotta mixture over cake mixture. Top with sliced apple.
7. Place crumble ingredients in a food processor and blitz until mixture resembles coarse breadcrumbs. Alternatively, use your fingers to rub butter through the dry ingredients. Sprinkle crumble topping evenly over cakes.
8. Bake for 25–30 minutes or until a skewer comes out clean. Cool before turning out. Garnish with mascarpone and Dried Apple Slices.

Dried Apple Slices

In a bowl, combine 1 tablespoon caster sugar, juice of 1 lemon and a splash of water. Toss one cored and finely sliced Granny Smith apple in the sugar mixture. Arrange apple slices in a single layer on a lined baking tray and cook in an oven preheated to 50°C for 30 minutes, until dry.

Kitchen Notes

New Zealand-made walnut paste is available from specialty food stores.

little and friday.

Portuguese Custard Tarts

These tarts are best eaten on the day they are baked.

1 recipe Flaky Pastry (see page 182)

Custard
⅔ cup caster sugar
⅔ cup water
4 cups milk
4 tbsp cornflour
7 egg yolks
1 tsp vanilla extract
⅓ cup caster sugar, for sprinkling

Makes 12 tarts

1. To make custard, place first measure of sugar and the water in a heavy-based saucepan over medium heat. Bring to the boil, then reduce heat and simmer for 5 minutes.
2. Add ½ cup milk to cornflour and mix to a smooth paste.
3. Place egg yolks, vanilla and remaining 3½ cups milk in a bowl and whisk to combine. Add cornflour paste and whisk until smooth.
4. Slowly pour sugar syrup into the milk mixture, whisking as you pour. Return mixture to the saucepan and stir continuously with a wooden spoon over low heat until mixture begins to bubble and coats the back of the spoon.
5. Remove custard from heat and pour into a bowl. Cover with cling film. Cool and refrigerate overnight to set.
6. To assemble tarts, on a lightly floured bench roll out pastry to 2mm thick. Using a 10cm-diameter cookie cutter, cut out 24 circles. Using a pastry brush, lightly brush the pastry circles with cold water. Sprinkle with caster sugar to coat.
7. Stack two pastry circles on top of each other to form 12 circles. Using a rolling pin, roll the circles again to 3mm thick and a little wider than 10cm in diameter.
8. Grease and line a 12-hole patty tray with pastry, trimming the edges so the pastry sits 1cm above the top of the tin. Refrigerate for 30 minutes.
9. Preheat oven to 200°C. Spoon prepared custard into pastry cases to three-quarters fill them.
10. Bake in centre of oven for 25–30 minutes. Cool for 10 minutes before easing tarts out of tins with a palette knife.
11. Sprinkle 1 teaspoon caster sugar over each tart, and use a cook's blowtorch to melt the sugar until golden. Alternatively, place tarts under a hot grill for a few minutes.

Blood Orange Baby Cakes

If you wish, you can boost the orange flavour of these moist cakes by adding more rind to the syrup.

125g unsalted butter

1 cup caster sugar

3 eggs

1 cup flour

1 tsp baking powder

¼ cup ground almonds

½ cup sour cream

zest and juice of 4 blood oranges

Orange Syrup

½ cup caster sugar

zest and juice of 3 blood oranges

Icing

3 tbsp frozen raspberries

½ cup icing sugar

Candied Orange Peel, to decorate (see page 186)

edible flowers, to decorate

Makes 12 small cakes

1. Preheat oven to 180°C. Grease and line 12 dariole moulds or a 12-hole muffin tray with baking paper.
2. Using an electric mixer, beat butter and sugar until pale and fluffy. Add eggs one at a time, mixing well after each addition.
3. Sift flour and baking powder into a bowl and add ground almonds. Using a large metal spoon, fold flour mixture through creamed mixture. Lastly fold in sour cream and orange zest and juice.
4. Spoon mixture into prepared tins. Bake in oven for 15–20 minutes or until a skewer comes out clean.
5. While cakes are cooking, make the Orange Syrup by combining sugar and orange zest and juice in a saucepan over medium heat. Stir until sugar dissolves.
6. Turn out cakes while they are still warm. Pour syrup into a shallow dish and roll cakes in the syrup to coat.
7. To make the icing, blitz raspberries and icing sugar in a food processor to combine. Pour icing over cakes while they are still warm. Decorate with a strip of Candied Orange Peel and an edible flower, such as a pansy.

little and friday.

EASTER

On a beautiful crisp autumn morning we gathered for a laid-back outdoor Easter brunch. We hid the boxes of chocolate goodies throughout the garden and handed out hand-drawn maps to keep the children busy while we fired up the barbecue. It is essential to bake all breads on the day; this can mean an early start, but it is well worth it. Make your sweet treats the day before. The Chocolate Rochers are best made once the kids are in bed!

Tomato and Egg Bake

Spinach and Feta-topped Turkish Pide

Breakfast Galette

Banana and Plum Jam

Homemade Herb Butter

Hot Cross Buns

Hot Cross Bun and Butter Pudding

Chocolate Chilli Easter Donuts

Chocolate Rochers

Tomato and Egg Bake

This simple breakfast dish can be cooked on a barbecue
or the stovetop.

2 tbsp extra virgin olive oil
1 onion, finely chopped
3 cloves garlic, crushed
2 × 400g cans chopped
tomatoes or 1kg fresh tomatoes
2 tbsp chopped fresh oregano
salt and freshly ground pepper
5 eggs

Serves 5

1. Heat oil in a heavy-based frying pan. Add onion and garlic
   and cook over medium heat for 5 minutes.
2. Add tomatoes and oregano and season with salt and pepper.
   Cook for 30 minutes over low heat.
3. Using a spoon, create five cavities in the tomato mixture
   and crack an egg into each cavity. Cook until eggs are just
   poached, approximately 5–10 minutes. Serve with bread.

Spinach and Feta-topped Turkish Pide

A simple twist on our Turkish Pide and perfect for brunch.

1 recipe Turkish Pide (see
page 16)
½ cup chopped walnuts
4 cups baby spinach
¼ cup water
200g feta, crumbled

Makes 2 loaves

1. Prepare Turkish Pide by following recipe from steps 1–4.
2. Preheat oven to 160°C. Place walnuts on a baking tray and
   roast for 10 minutes.
3. Increase oven temperature to 260°C.
4. Place spinach in a saucepan with water and cook over
   medium heat for a few minutes to wilt the spinach. Cool and
   squeeze excess moisture from the spinach.
5. Top pide loaves with spinach, feta and walnuts. Bake for 6–8
   minutes until edges of loaves are a mottled pale-golden colour.

Caramelised Onion Pide

Prepare Turkish Pide by following recipe from steps 1–5. Top pide
loaves with 2 cups Onion Jam (see page 186) and 200g crumbled
feta. Bake in a preheated 260°C oven for 6–8 minutes.

little and friday.

Breakfast Galette

A classic big breakfast – on pastry.

1 sheet Flaky Pastry (see page 182)

Topping
1 cup Rocket Pesto (see page 185)
250g baby spinach leaves
¼ cup water
Thyme Mushrooms (see below)
6 eggs
10 vine-ripened tomatoes
6 rashers bacon
chives, to garnish

Egg Wash
2 eggs
2 tbsp cream

Thyme Mushrooms
3 tbsp unsalted butter
2 cloves garlic, chopped
2 tbsp thyme leaves
300g button mushrooms, sliced
zest and juice of 1 lemon
salt and freshly ground pepper

Makes one 28cm galette

1. Cut a 28cm-diameter circle from the pastry sheet and place on a lined baking tray. Rest in refrigerator for 20 minutes.
2. Preheat oven to 200°C.
3. Remove pastry base from refrigerator. Using a sharp knife, score a line 2.5cm in from the edge to create a border, taking care not to cut right through pastry.
4. Make egg wash by mixing together the eggs and cream. Using a pastry brush, paint the pastry disk with egg wash. Then spread pastry with a thick layer of pesto, inside the border.
5. Place baby spinach in a saucepan with water and cook over high heat for a few minutes to wilt. Cool, then squeeze out excess moisture from the spinach.
6. Top galette with spinach, leaving a narrow rim of pastry around the edge, and scatter Thyme Mushrooms over. Form six cavities in the spinach and mushrooms, and crack an egg into each cavity. Scatter tomatoes over.
7. Cook galette in centre of oven for 20–30 minutes until pastry crust is golden.
8. Meanwhile, place bacon on a tray and cook in oven for 10 minutes.
9. Garnish galette with cooked bacon and fresh chives.

Thyme Mushrooms
Melt butter in a frying pan and add garlic and thyme leaves. Cook for 1 minute. Add mushrooms and lemon zest and juice. Season with salt and pepper. Cook until mushrooms are soft.

Banana and Plum Jam

My mum got this recipe from Aunt Daisy in the 1950s.
It makes enough to last all year!

4kg good-quality red-flesh plums (e.g. Black Doris or Omega)
2 cups cold water
3.6kg caster sugar
55g unsalted butter
12 mashed bananas

Makes 30 × 230ml jars

1. Cut plums in half and remove stones.
2. Place plums and water in a large saucepan over medium heat. Stir until mixture boils. Turn down heat and simmer for 15 minutes until plums are soft.
3. Add half the sugar and boil over medium to high heat for 20 minutes. Add remaining sugar and the butter, and bring mixture to a gentle boil. Reduce heat and cook for 30 minutes. Add bananas and cook for a further 15 minutes. Remove from heat.
4. Meanwhile, wash 30 × 230ml jars with metal screw lids and place jars and lids on baking trays. Set oven to 150°C and place jars in oven for 20 minutes to sterilise. Remove from oven and fill with hot jam while jars are still warm. Place a circle of baking paper on top of the jam and screw lids on tightly. Label and date the jars and store in a cool, dark place for up to 12 months.

Homemade Herb Butter

If you have an electric mixer, it is easy to make your own butter.

1 litre cream
salt, to taste
2 tbsp finely chopped herbs

Makes 450g

1. Using an electric mixer, beat cream until it becomes a solid mass, leaving a milky whey. Drain off whey and wash butter mixture under cold water to remove any remaining whey.
2. Using a spoon, mix through salt and herbs until completely combined. Shape into a log and wrap in greaseproof paper. Refrigerate for up to two weeks.

little and friday.

Hot Cross Buns

Set the alarm for an early start so you can have these
for breakfast.

300ml milk
¼ cup caster sugar
5 cups high-grade flour
2 tbsp mixed spice
2 tbsp cinnamon
pinch of ground cloves
1 tsp salt
8 tsp instant dry yeast
1 egg, beaten
50g cold unsalted butter, diced
3 cups sultanas
½ cup mixed peel

For the crosses
½ cup water
½ cup flour

For the glaze
¼ cup caster sugar
½ cup water

Makes 12

1. In a small bowl place milk and sugar and stir to combine.
2. Place flour, spices, salt and yeast in a large bowl and stir to combine. Add milk mixture and egg to dry ingredients and mix to combine. Add butter and mix to combine.
3. Turn out onto a floured bench, and knead for approximately 10 minutes. Test the dough by pulling it apart. If it stretches and becomes transparent, it is ready to prove. If it breaks, continue kneading, then test again.
4. Add dried fruit to dough and knead until evenly combined. Cover bowl with a damp tea towel and leave to prove in a warm, draught-free place for 30–40 minutes until dough doubles in size.
5. On a floured bench, roll out dough to 4cm thick. Cut dough into 12 × 4cm squares. Cover with a damp tea towel and leave to prove for 20 minutes. Squash air out of dough and roll each piece into a ball shape.
6. Place balls 1cm apart on a lined baking tray and leave to prove until doubled in size, around 40 minutes.
7. Preheat oven to 180°C.
8. While buns are proving, make the flour paste for the crosses by mixing together flour and water. Place paste in a piping bag and, when buns have risen, pipe a cross onto each one.
9. Bake buns for 20 minutes or until golden. While hot, paint buns with glaze (see below).

Glaze
In a saucepan combine caster sugar and water. Boil over medium heat until sugar has dissolved.

Kitchen Notes
If using active dried yeast rather than instant dry yeast (see Helpful Hints, page 9), sprinkle 5 teaspoons over the milk and sugar mixture in step 1, and leave for 10 minutes before adding to the dry ingredients.

little and friday.

Hot Cross Bun and Butter Pudding

We created this recipe specially to use up leftover
Hot Cross Buns.

½ cup ground almonds or
hazelnuts

180g good-quality dark
chocolate, chopped

6 stale hot cross buns

6 dried figs, sliced

extra dark chocolate shavings,
to decorate

Custard

7 eggs

1 cup cream

2 cups milk

1 tsp vanilla extract

1 cup brown sugar

Crème Anglaise

250ml milk

¼ tsp vanilla paste

4 egg yolks

50g caster sugar

Makes 6

1. Preheat oven to 160°C. Grease and line sides and bottoms
   of a 6-hole Texas muffin tray with baking paper. Extend
   the baking paper 3cm above the rim of the tins so custard
   doesn't leak out. Place muffin tray on a baking tray to catch
   any overflow.
2. Place ground nuts and chocolate chunks in a bowl and toss to
   coat the chocolate.
3. Cut hot cross buns into 1cm-thick discs to fit the diameter of
   the muffin tins. Place a slice in the bottom of each prepared
   tin. Top with 1 tablespoon of chocolate and nut mixture and
   a slice of dried fig. Repeat to fill tins, finishing with a slice of
   bun and a slice of fig.
4. In a bowl, whisk together the custard ingredients until sugar
   has dissolved. Pour enough custard mixture over to cover
   each pudding and leave for 20 minutes so the bun slices
   absorb the custard. Top up with remaining custard.
5. Bake for 30–40 minutes. Leave for 20 minutes to cool and
   set. Turn puddings out, top with shavings of dark chocolate
   and serve with Crème Anglaise (see below).

Crème Anglaise

1. Place milk in a saucepan with vanilla paste and bring to the
   boil over medium heat. Remove from heat.
2. In a bowl, whisk egg yolks and sugar together until pale and
   creamy.
3. Gradually pour hot milk over the egg mixture, whisking
   continuously. Return to the saucepan and stir continuously
   over medium heat until mixture has thickened. Do not boil.
4. Remove from heat and immerse the base of the saucepan in a
   sink of cold water to halt cooking.
5. Pour Créme Anglaise into a container, cover and store in the
   refrigerator for up to three days. When ready to serve, warm
   in a saucepan over low heat.

little and friday.

Chocolate Chilli Easter Donuts

Omit the chilli from the cream filling if your kids don't like it.

Donut Dough

3 cups flour

¼ cup caster sugar

2 tsp instant dry yeast

1½ tsp salt

180ml milk, at room temperature

1 large egg plus 2 egg yolks

100g unsalted butter

4 cups coconut oil, for frying

1 recipe Chocolate Chilli Cream (see below)

1 recipe Vanilla Sugar (see opposite)

Chocolate Chilli Cream

500ml milk

1 tsp vanilla paste

½ cup caster sugar

3 egg yolks

¼ cup cornflour

500g good-quality dark chocolate, grated

¼ cup good-quality cocoa

pinch of chilli powder (optional)

1 tsp cinnamon

Makes 10

1. Place flour, sugar, yeast and salt into the bowl of an electric mixer. Using a dough hook, mix at low speed to combine. Alternatively, mix by hand.
2. Add milk, egg and egg yolks. Continue mixing on low speed until a sticky dough forms. Increase speed to medium and continue kneading for 3–4 minutes. If doing this by hand, tip dough onto a lightly floured bench and knead for 10 minutes.
3. Gradually add butter one piece at a time, ensuring each piece is combined before adding the next. This will take about 12 minutes in a mixer. When all butter is well combined, stop the mixer and test the dough by pulling it apart. If it stretches and becomes transparent, it is ready to prove. If it breaks, continue mixing and test again.
4. Place dough in bowl and cover with a damp tea towel. Leave in a warm, draught-free place to prove until doubled in size.
5. Tip dough onto a floured bench and roll out to 3cm thick. Leave for a few minutes, as the dough will shrink a little then spring back.
6. Using a 6.5cm oval-shaped cookie cutter, cut out 10 donuts. Place on a lined baking tray and rest for 20 minutes until the dough feels light and fluffy when pressed.
7. To cook donuts, in a large, deep frying pan heat coconut oil to 180°C on a candy thermometer. Cook 4 donuts at a time for 2 minutes on each side. Remove with a slotted spoon and toss in Vanilla Sugar while hot. Allow to cool before filling with Chocolate Chilli Cream by poking a hole into each donut with a sharp knife to create a cavity. Fill a piping bag with Chocolate Chilli Cream and fill donuts until they expand slightly. Tie with ribbon.

Chocolate Chilli Cream
Makes 3 cups

1. In a saucepan combine milk, vanilla paste and ¼ cup sugar. Bring to the boil.

little and friday.

2. Meanwhile, using an electric mixer, whisk remaining ¼ cup sugar, egg yolks and cornflour until pale and thick.

3. Slowly pour a third of the milk mixture into the egg mixture with the mixer on low speed.

4. Return remaining milk mixture to the heat and bring to the boil. Quickly add egg yolk mixture to hot milk mixture, whisking constantly. It is a real workout but if you don't whisk vigorously you will have a lumpy cream. Keep whisking until it boils. Remove from heat.

5. Melt chocolate in a glass bowl over a saucepan of simmering water. Add cocoa,

chilli powder (if using) and cinnamon and stir to combine. Cool mixture until the same temperature as the egg mixture.

6. Add egg mixture to chocolate and stir to combine. Chocolate Chilli Cream will keep covered in the refrigerator for three days. Remove from refrigerator before using and beat the cream until smooth.

Vanilla Sugar

In a bowl combine 1½ cups caster sugar, ½ tsp vanilla extract and a pinch of salt. Use your fingers to work the vanilla paste into the sugar. Tip onto a tray and rest in a warm place, such as a hot-water cupboard, to dry out.

Easter

Chocolate Rochers

These are so easy to make. You can use any kind of nuts,
or shredded coconut to create coconut rough.

150g slivered almonds
⅓ cup icing sugar
1 tsp vanilla extract
750g good-quality dark
chocolate, chopped

Makes 12

1. Preheat oven to 180°C. Line a tray with baking paper.
2. In a bowl, combine almonds, icing sugar and vanilla. Toss to coat nuts, then spread mixture onto lined baking tray.
3. Bake for 10 minutes, or until golden brown. Take care the almonds do not burn.
4. Melt chocolate in a glass bowl over a saucepan of simmering water.
5. Tip almonds into chocolate and stir to combine. Place teaspoonfuls onto lined baking tray and leave to set.

Kitchen Notes
I recommend using Whittaker's 50% Cocoa chocolate for this recipe, as it is already tempered.

CHOCOLATE 21ST

For years now I have made cakes for 21st birthdays, and chocolate is always the most popular choice. Actually, chocolate tends to be the most popular choice for all age groups! Here we have created a chocolate banquet, with lots of variations on the tried and true, including a rich gluten-free option. We've added some different presentation ideas too, to give you extra inspiration.

Chocolate, Beetroot and Salted Caramel Cake

Cinnamon Chai Bundt Cake

Fig and Chocolate Cake

Chocolate Sour Cream Bundt Cake

Macadamia Chocolate Cake

Zucchini and Chocolate Cake

Pear and Pistachio Chocolate Cake

Chocolate, Beetroot and Salted Caramel Cake

This flavour combination is sensational.

5 eggs

2½ cups caster sugar

300ml canola oil

250g good-quality dark chocolate, chopped

2 cups flour

1 cup good-quality cocoa

2 tsp baking powder

100ml milk

1 cup grated raw beetroot

3 cups Chocolate Ganache, to decorate (see page 187)

Salted Caramel

1½ cups caster sugar

300ml cream

½ tsp sea salt

Makes one 23cm triple-layer cake

1. Preheat oven to 160°C. Grease and line three 23cm round cake tins with baking paper.
2. Using an electric mixer, whisk eggs and sugar on medium speed until mixture is pale and creamy and tripled in volume. With mixer on medium speed, slowly drizzle in oil and combine.
3. Melt chocolate in a glass bowl over a saucepan of simmering water. Add chocolate to egg mixture. Stir to combine.
4. Sift flour, cocoa and baking powder into a bowl. Using a large metal spoon, fold a third of the dry ingredients into chocolate mixture. Add a third of the milk and combine. Continue in this way until all combined.
5. Fold grated beetroot through chocolate mixture.
6. Spoon mixture into prepared tins. Bake in centre of oven for 40 minutes or until a skewer comes out clean. Cool in tins before turning out.
7. To assemble, use a serrated knife to cut the domed tops off the cakes. Spread ½ cup Salted Caramel over the top of two cakes and stack to form one triple-layer cake sandwiched together with caramel.
8. Spread a thick layer of Chocolate Ganache over top and sides of cake using a palette knife.

Salted Caramel
Makes 1½ cups

1. Place sugar in a small saucepan and just cover with water to achieve a wet-sand consistency.
2. Bring to the boil but do not stir. Using a wet pastry brush, remove any sugar crystals from sides of saucepan. Continue to boil until mixture turns amber. Remove from heat.
3. In a small saucepan, heat cream to boiling point. Gradually add to caramelised sugar, stirring constantly until smooth. This takes a while but eventually combines. Season with salt.

little and friday.

Cinnamon Chai Bundt Cake

This recipe is based on one from Rose Levy Beranbaum's
The Cake Bible. I have spiced it up with chai.

Crumble Filling

1 cup chopped dates

2 chai tea bags, to infuse

1 cup brown sugar

1 cup walnuts

1 tbsp good-quality cocoa

3 tsp cinnamon, plus 1 tsp extra
for dusting tin

4 tsp chai powder (from chai
tea bags)

150g good-quality dark
chocolate, chopped

Cake

1 cup sour cream

½ cup yoghurt

1½ tsp baking soda

3 cups flour, plus extra for
dusting tin

1 tsp ground ginger

2 tsp baking powder

½ tsp salt

250g unsalted butter

1¼ cups caster sugar

3 eggs

1 tbsp chai syrup

2 tsp vanilla extract

1 cup Chocolate Ganache
(see page 187)

Makes one 25cm cake

1. Preheat oven to 180°C. Grease a 25cm bundt cake tin and
   dust with ¼ cup flour mixed with 1 teaspoon cinnamon.
   Tap to remove excess.
2. To make crumble filling, place dates and 2 chai tea bags in a
   saucepan with 1½ cups water. Simmer for 5–10 minutes until
   liquid is absorbed. Cool.
3. Place remaining ingredients into a food processor, and pulse
   until mixture resembles breadcrumbs. Add cooked dates and
   pulse to combine.
4. To make cake, place sour cream and yoghurt in a bowl and
   mix to combine. Mix in baking soda. Leave mixture for
   15 minutes.
5. Meanwhile, sift flour, ginger, baking powder and salt into a
   bowl and set aside.
6. In an electric mixer, beat butter and sugar until pale and
   fluffy. Add eggs one at a time, mixing well after each addition.
   Add chai syrup and vanilla and mix to combine.
7. Using a large metal spoon, fold a third of the dry ingredients
   into creamed mixture, followed by a third of the sour cream
   mixture. Continue in this way until all combined.
8. Spread a quarter of the cake mixture into the prepared
   tin and top with a third of the crumble filling. Repeat the
   process, finishing with a layer of cake mixture.
9. Bake in centre of oven for 40 minutes or until a skewer
   comes out clean. Remove from oven and cool in tin.
10. Before turning cake out, use a serrated knife to trim the top
    flush with the tin.
11. Gently warm Chocolate Ganache and drizzle over cake.

Kitchen Notes
Chai syrup is available from specialty food stores.

little and friday.

Fig and Chocolate Cake

A delicious gluten-free cake that keeps well.

1½ cups chopped dried figs

3 cups hazelnuts

250g good-quality dark chocolate, chopped

250g unsalted butter

1½ cups caster sugar

6 eggs

½ cup ground almonds

To assemble

2 cups Chocolate Ganache (see page 187)

½ cup compound chocolate

6 fresh figs, halved

Makes one 23cm cake

1. Preheat oven to 160°C. Grease and line a 23cm round cake tin with baking paper.
2. Place dried figs in a saucepan with 1 cup water and simmer over low heat for 10 minutes. Cool.
3. Place hazelnuts on a baking tray and roast for 10 minutes. Remove hazelnut skins by rubbing in a tea towel. Coarsely grind hazelnuts in a food processor.
4. Melt chocolate in a double boiler or in a bowl over a saucepan of simmering water. Cool.
5. Using an electric mixer, beat butter and sugar until pale and fluffy. Add eggs one at a time, beating well after each addition. Add cooked figs, ground hazelnuts, melted chocolate and ground almonds and stir to combine. Spread mixture into prepared tin.
6. Bake in centre of oven for 55 minutes or until a skewer comes out clean. Cool in tin before turning out.
7. To assemble, spread top and sides of cake with Chocolate Ganache.
8. To make chocolate lace, melt compound chocolate slowly in a glass bowl over a saucepan of simmering water. Place melted chocolate in a piping bag. On a sheet of baking paper trace around the 23cm cake tin and pipe a chocolate lace design inside the circle. Leave to set.
9. Arrange 9 fig halves around top of cake. Using two knives, carefully remove chocolate lace from baking paper and place on top of cake. Carefully place remaining fig halves on top of chocolate lace.

Chocolate Sour Cream Bundt Cake

This makes a rich chocolate cake in a spectacular shape.

200g good-quality dark chocolate, chopped

1 cup good-quality cocoa, plus extra for dusting

1 cup boiling water

280g unsalted butter

2½ cups brown sugar

6 eggs

2 tsp vanilla extract

2½ cups flour

1½ tsp baking powder

pinch of salt

1½ cups sour cream

1½ cups good-quality dark chocolate chips

1 cup Chocolate Ganache, to decorate (see page 187)

Makes one 25cm cake

1. Preheat oven to 160°C. Grease a 25cm bundt tin and dust with ¼ cup cocoa. Tap out the excess cocoa.
2. Melt chocolate in a glass bowl over a saucepan of simmering water. Add 1 cup cocoa and boiling water and stir to combine. Set aside to cool.
3. Using an electric mixer, beat butter and sugar until pale and creamy. Add eggs one at a time, mixing well after each addition. Add vanilla and mix to combine. Scrape down sides of bowl.
4. Using a large metal spoon, fold melted chocolate through creamed butter mixture.
5. Sift flour, baking powder and salt into a bowl. Using a large metal spoon, fold dry ingredients into chocolate mixture. Fold sour cream through, followed by chocolate chips.
6. Spoon mixture into bundt tin and cook in centre of oven for 60–65 minutes or until a skewer comes out clean. Cool in tin.
7. Before turning cake out, use a serrated knife to trim the top flush with the tin. Gently warm Chocolate Ganache to pouring consistency and pour over cake.

Macadamia Chocolate Cake

You can exchange the macadamias for hazelnuts.

400g good-quality dark chocolate, chopped

100g unsalted butter

1 cup macadamia nuts

3 eggs

1 cup firmly packed brown sugar

50ml strong coffee

1¼ cups flour

2½ tsp baking powder

¼ cup good-quality cocoa

¼ cup milk

To decorate

2 cups Chocolate Ganache (see page 187)

Candied Macadamias (see below)

Candied Macadamias

1 cup caster sugar

50ml water

10 macadamia nuts

Makes one 18cm double-layer cake

1. Preheat oven to 180°C. Grease and line two 18cm round cake tins with baking paper.
2. Place chocolate and butter in a glass bowl over a saucepan of simmering water. Melt and stir to combine.
3. Place macadamia nuts on a baking tray and roast in oven for 10 minutes. Cool before roughly chopping in a food processor.
4. Using an electric mixer, whisk eggs and sugar until pale and fluffy and mixture has tripled in volume. With the mixer on slow speed, slowly add chocolate mixture and coffee and beat to combine.
5. Sift flour, baking powder and cocoa into a bowl. Using a large metal spoon, fold a third of the dry ingredients through the chocolate mixture, then fold through a third of the milk. Repeat until all combined. Lastly, fold chopped nuts through the mixture.
6. Spoon mixture into prepared tins and bake in centre of oven for 35 minutes or until a skewer comes out clean. Cool cakes in tins before turning out. Lower oven temperature to 150°C.
7. Using a serrated knife, cut domed tops off cakes and blitz the tops in a food processor to fine breadcrumbs. Bake crumbs on a lined oven tray for 10 minutes.
8. To assemble cake, spread top of one cake with a thick layer of Chocolate Ganache. Place second cake on top, and spread top and sides with remaining ganache. Cover with cake crumbs and decorate with Candied Macadamias.

Candied Macadamias

1. Place sugar and water in a heavy-based saucepan over medium heat. Bring to the boil and cook, without stirring, until mixture turns an amber colour.
2. Remove from heat and immerse base of saucepan in a sink of cold water for 2 minutes to cool and thicken mixture.
3. Insert a bamboo skewer into each macadamia nut. Dip nuts into the caramel, allowing excess caramel to drip off and

little and friday.

form a point. You can do this by taping the end of each skewer to the edge of a bench so the nuts are suspended in midair. Place newspaper on the floor below to catch drips of caramel. If the caramel hardens in the pan, reheat over a low heat to soften.

Kitchen Notes

The Candied Macadamias need to be made on the day of serving.

Zucchini and Chocolate Cake

This is a moist cake that lasts for days. You can substitute
white chocolate when making the decorative spikes, if desired.

180g good-quality dark
chocolate, chopped

50g dark chocolate bits

2 cups flour

½ cup good-quality cocoa

2 tsp baking powder

4 eggs

2 cups caster sugar

300ml canola oil

1 tsp vanilla

50ml strong coffee

2 cups grated zucchini

100ml cream

To assemble

3 cups Chocolate Ganache
(see page 187)

Chocolate Spikes (see below)

Makes one 18cm double-layer cake

1. Preheat oven to 180°C. Grease and line two 18cm round tins
   with baking paper.
2. Melt chocolate in a glass bowl over a saucepan of simmering
   water. Cool.
3. Toss chocolate bits in 1 tablespoon of the flour and set aside.
4. Sift flour, cocoa and baking powder into a bowl and set aside.
5. Using an electric mixer, whisk eggs and sugar until mixture
   is pale and creamy and tripled in volume. With mixer on
   medium speed, slowly drizzle in oil and combine.
6. Add melted chocolate, vanilla and coffee and mix to combine.
7. Using a large metal spoon, fold dry ingredients into chocolate
   mixture. Fold grated zucchini and chocolate bits through
   mixture. Lastly, fold through the cream.
8. Spoon mixture into prepared tins and bake in centre of oven
   for 40 minutes or until a skewer comes out clean. Cool in tins
   before turning out.
9. To assemble, use a serrated knife to cut the domed tops off
   the cakes. Spread a thick layer of Chocolate Ganache over
   one cake and top with second cake. Spread top and sides of
   cake with ganache, using a palette knife, before decorating
   with Chocolate Spikes.

Chocolate Spikes

Melt 350g compound chocolate in a glass bowl over a saucepan
of simmering water. Pour melted chocolate onto a tray lined with
baking paper. Use a palette knife to spread chocolate to 2mm
thick. Allow chocolate to semi-set. Using a sharp paring knife, cut
chocolate into long spikes. Cool completely before placing around
circumference of cake, pressing into ganache to secure.

Pear and Pistachio Chocolate Cake

Golden pear slices are a delicious accompaniment to this cake.

200g good-quality dark chocolate, chopped
½ cup pistachios
150g unsalted butter
½ cup caster sugar
3 eggs
1 cup flour
1 tsp baking powder
1 pear, grated

To decorate
1 cup Chocolate Ganache (see page 187)
Caramelised Pears (see below)

Caramelised Pears
1 tbsp unsalted butter
¼ cup caster sugar
2 ripe pears
¼ cup manuka honey

Makes one 23cm cake

1. Preheat oven to 160°C. Grease and line a 23cm round cake tin with baking paper.
2. Blitz chocolate and pistachios in a food processor until mixture resembles breadcrumbs.
3. Using an electric mixer, beat butter and sugar until pale and fluffy. Add eggs one at a time, beating well after each addition.
4. Using a large metal spoon, fold ground chocolate and pistachio mixture into creamed mixture.
5. Sift flour and baking powder into a separate bowl and fold through chocolate mixture. Lastly, fold grated pear through mixture until just combined.
6. Spoon mixture into prepared tin and bake in centre of oven for 40 minutes or until a skewer comes out clean. Cool in tin before turning out.
7. Spread top and sides of cake with Chocolate Ganache and decorate with Caramelised Pears.

Caramelised Pears

1. Place butter and sugar in a frying pan over medium heat and cook, stirring, until sugar dissolves (1–2 minutes).
2. Slice pears into 2cm-thick slices, leaving stalk intact, and add to frying pan. Cook until soft (10–20 minutes). Add honey and cook for 3 minutes. Cool before using.

Kitchen Notes
We also like to serve this cake cut crosswise into two layers, filled with Chocolate Ganache and slices of Caramelised Pears.

BASICS

These recipes are the foundation of many of our creations. They are staple items in our pantry at Little and Friday, and as many of them will keep in the freezer or pantry, there's no harm in having them on hand.

Sweet Pastry

Flaky Pastry

Buns for Hot Dogs and Sliders

Brioche Dough

Aïoli

Pizza Dough

Rocket Pesto

Balsamic Reduction

Candied Orange Peel

Onion Jam

Roasted Garlic

Chocolate Cookie Dough

Chocolate Ganache

Crème Pâtissière

Crème Diplomat

Sweet Pastry

2¾ cups flour
1 cup icing sugar
pinch of salt
250g unsalted butter
1 egg
1 tsp lemon juice
½ tsp lemon zest
vanilla extract or paste, to taste

1. In a food processor, combine flour, icing sugar and salt and pulse in 2-second bursts to aerate and combine.
2. Add butter and pulse until mixture resembles breadcrumbs.
3. Add egg, lemon juice, zest and vanilla and pulse 10 times. The mixture should look dry and crumbly.
4. Turn out onto a clean work surface and gather mixture together with your hands. Gently shape mixture into a ball.
5. Wrap in cling film and refrigerate for 2 hours before using.

Flaky Pastry

Makes 2 sheets

3 cups flour
pinch of salt
450g unsalted butter, frozen
180ml iced water

1. Sift flour and salt into a large bowl. Grate 180g butter into bowl and, using your fingers, work into flour.
2. Dice remaining butter into 1cm cubes and add to bowl. Lightly mix with your hands until butter cubes are coated with flour mixture.
3. Add iced water and mix with your hands until dough starts to come together. (The mixture will be studded with large lumps of butter and quite dry at this point.)
4. Tip mixture onto a floured bench and gently work together with your hands to form a rough ball.
5. Roll out to a 30cm × 20cm rectangle. With the long side facing you, fold short sides to meet at the centre. Fold in half again.
6. Wrap in cling film and chill in refrigerator for at least 2 hours, or ideally overnight.
7. Roll into a 30cm × 20cm rectangle and fold as before. Do this twice, then return to refrigerator for 30 minutes to rest.
8. Cut pastry in half. On a floured bench roll each half out to a 30cm × 35cm × 6mm thick sheet. Best used within 24 hours.

Kitchen Notes
Pastry must be kept cool, so no hot hands or equipment. The longer you leave your pastry to rest in between rolls and folds, the flakier it will be.

little and friday.

Buns for Hot Dogs and Sliders

2 cups high-grade flour, plus extra for dusting

2 tsp caster sugar

1½ tsp instant dry yeast

1 tsp salt

¾ cup water

2 tbsp unsalted butter

sesame seeds, for sprinkling on slider buns

Makes 24 small buns

1. Combine flour, sugar, yeast and salt in an electric mixer with a dough hook attachment. Add water and butter and knead for 10 minutes on medium speed. Alternatively, stir mixture with a wooden spoon to combine and knead for 15 minutes by hand.
2. Place dough in an oiled mixing bowl and cover with a damp tea towel, making sure the tea towel does not touch the dough. Leave in a warm, draught-free place for 1 hour, or until dough has doubled in size.
3. Turn dough out onto a floured bench and knock out the air with a few good thumps. Cover dough again and rest for 20–30 minutes.
4. Divide dough into 24 pieces. With the palm of your hand roll each piece into a ball. Cover and rest for 30 minutes.

To make slider buns

1. Reroll each dough ball into a perfect ball shape. Press flat to form a disc approximately 5cm in diameter by 2cm thick.
2. Place on lined baking trays. Lightly brush buns with water and sprinkle with sesame seeds.
3. Cover with a damp tea towel and rest for a further 30–60 minutes
4. Preheat oven to 220°C. Bake buns for 10 minutes until golden. Cool on a wire rack.

To make hot dog buns

1. Using the palm of your hand, roll each dough ball into an even log shape, approximately 10cm long.
2. Place on lined baking trays, cover with a damp tea towel and rest for 30–60 minutes.
3. Preheat oven to 220°C. Bake buns for 10–15 minutes until golden. Cool on a wire rack.

Brioche Dough

550ml milk

60g fresh yeast, crumbled (or 3 tsp instant dry yeast)

6½ cups flour

3 tsp salt

½ cup caster sugar

3 eggs

140g unsalted butter, diced

1. In a saucepan, heat milk over a medium heat until lukewarm. Remove from heat and sprinkle yeast over. Stir until yeast has dissolved.
2. Place dry ingredients in a mixing bowl. Using an electric beater with dough hook attachment, mix at low speed.
3. Add yeast mixture and eggs to bowl, continuing to mix at low speed. Mix until a sticky dough forms.
4. Stop mixer and scrape down dough from sides of bowl. Increase to medium speed and mix for 10 minutes until an elastic, shiny dough forms that pulls away from the bowl. If doing this by hand, tip dough onto bench and knead for 10 minutes.
5. Gradually add butter to dough mixture, mixing until well combined.
6. Cover bowl with a tea towel and leave dough to prove until it has almost doubled in size. Tip dough onto a floured bench. It is now ready to use.

Kitchen Notes

The proving, or rising, of the dough is highly dependent on the room temperature. If you find it is proving too quickly, you can place it in the refrigerator for short periods to slow down the process.

Aïoli

2–3 cloves garlic, chopped

2 egg yolks

pinch of salt and freshly ground pepper, to taste

1 cup extra virgin olive oil

2 tbsp lemon juice

1 tsp Dijon mustard

Makes ½ cup

1. Place the garlic, egg yolks and seasoning in a food processor and blitz until well combined.
2. With the motor running, slowly add the oil, being careful not to add it too quickly or the mixture may separate. If you are making this by hand, use a hand whisk. Mix until thick.
3. Add the lemon juice and mustard and mix until combined. Will keep covered in the refrigerator for up to two weeks.

Pizza Dough

500g flour
2 tbsp extra virgin olive oil
300ml cold water
3½ tsp instant dry yeast (or 20g fresh yeast)
pinch of salt

Makes 8 × thin 23cm pizza bases

1. Place flour in a bowl. Make a well in the centre and add oil, water, yeast and salt. Using your hands, bring mixture together to form a sticky dough.
2. Turn out onto a heavily floured bench and knead for 10 minutes, until the dough becomes smooth. If using an electric mixer with a dough hook, knead for 4–5 minutes.
3. Form dough into a ball and place in an oiled bowl. Cover with a damp tea towel and leave to double in size.
4. Turn dough out onto floured bench and cut into 8 pieces. Using the palm of your hand, roll each piece into a ball. Cover with a damp tea towel and rest for 10–15 minutes.
5. Roll out each ball of dough into a circle about 23cm in diameter and 3mm thick. (You want it to be very thin so it cooks in the middle and forms a crisp pizza crust.)

Rocket Pesto

1½ cups rocket
1½ cups walnuts
4 cloves garlic
4 tbsp extra virgin olive oil
salt and freshly ground pepper

Makes approx. 1 cup

Combine rocket, walnuts and garlic in a food processor and blitz to combine. Slowly add olive oil and process until just combined but still chunky. Season to taste. Refrigerate for up to two weeks.

Balsamic Reduction

1½ cups balsamic vinegar
½ cup honey
1 tbsp caster sugar

Makes approx. 1 cup

Combine balsamic vinegar, honey and sugar in a saucepan over a medium heat and boil for approximately 10 minutes until mixture is reduced by half and looks like treacle. Store in a screwtop jar in a dark, dry place for up to two weeks.

Candied Orange Peel

peel of 10 oranges
3 cups caster sugar

1. Place orange peel in a saucepan with enough cold water to cover and bring to the boil. Drain, then repeat this process.
2. Place drained orange peel and 2 cups sugar in saucepan with enough cold water to cover and bring to the boil. Reduce heat to low and simmer until the peel is almost translucent. Keep checking water level to make sure it doesn't boil dry.
3. Remove from heat, drain and leave to cool. Transfer to a tray lined with baking paper and leave to dry overnight.
4. The following day, dip the pieces of orange peel in the remaining 1 cup caster sugar to coat. Store in an airtight container for up to two weeks.

Onion Jam

2 tbsp extra virgin olive oil
3 cloves garlic, chopped
50g unsalted butter
¼ cup brown sugar
¼ cup balsamic vinegar
4 red onions, sliced
2 tbsp chopped thyme leaves
salt and freshly ground pepper

Makes 1 cup

1. In a heavy-based saucepan, heat the olive oil over medium heat and cook the garlic for a couple of minutes, but do not brown. Add butter, sugar and vinegar and combine before adding onions and thyme.
2. Turn heat to low and cook for approximately 25 minutes, stirring frequently to prevent mixture sticking to the bottom of the pan. Season with salt and pepper.
3. Cool before spooning into an airtight container. Onion Jam will keep for up to two weeks in the refrigerator.

Roasted Garlic

1 garlic bulb

Makes 1 bulb

1. Preheat oven to 150°C.
2. Soak garlic bulb in cold water for 20 minutes, then drain and wrap in tinfoil. Bake for 30 minutes or until soft. Cool.

Chocolate Cookie Dough

3 cups flour
¾ cup good-quality cocoa
½ tsp salt
225g unsalted butter
1 cup caster sugar
½ cup brown sugar
1 tsp vanilla extract
2 eggs

1. In a bowl, sift together flour, cocoa and salt.
2. Using an electric mixer, beat butter and both sugars until pale and fluffy (approximately 5 minutes), regularly scraping down the sides of the bowl. Add vanilla and mix to combine.
3. Add eggs one at a time, making sure each egg is well combined before adding the next. Scrape down the sides of the bowl and beat mixture a further 1 minute.
4. Using a metal spoon, fold dry ingredients through and mix until just combined. Do not overmix.
5. Turn dough onto a lightly floured bench and gently work into a ball with your hands. Wrap in cling film and chill in the refrigerator overnight or for up to one week.

Kitchen Notes
Cut out cookies in advance and store in the refrigerator on trays wrapped in cling film, then bake as required.

Chocolate Ganache

½ cup cream
200g good-quality dark chocolate, grated

Makes 1 cup
In a saucepan, heat cream to just below boiling point. Remove from heat and stir in chocolate until melted and smooth. Allow to cool and thicken before using.

Kitchen Notes
The ganache can be made a day in advance and stored in a cool place. Do not refrigerate. You can increase this recipe by using the same ratio of cream to chocolate. For 2 cups use 1 cup cream and 400g chocolate. For 3 cups use 1½ cups cream and 600g chocolate. For 4 cups use 2 cups cream and 800g chocolate.

Crème Pâtissière

500ml milk
1 tsp vanilla essence
½ cup caster sugar
3 egg yolks
¼ cup cornflour

Makes 2½ cups

1. In a saucepan, combine milk, vanilla and ¼ cup caster sugar, and bring to the boil.
2. In a bowl, beat together remaining caster sugar, egg yolks and cornflour until mixture is pale and thick.
3. Whisking constantly at low speed, slowly pour half the milk mixture into the egg mixture.
4. Return remaining milk to the heat and quickly add egg yolk mixture to milk, beating constantly. It is a real workout, but if you don't beat it vigorously enough the Crème Pâtissière will be lumpy. Keep beating the mixture over the heat until it comes back to the boil, then remove from the heat, pour into a bowl and cover with cling film. Cool before using.

Kitchen Notes

Crème Pâtissière may be kept refrigerated for up to three days. Before using, beat with a wooden spoon, or in an electric mixer, to bring it back to a smooth consistency.

Crème Diplomat

1 cup cream
1 cup Crème Pâtissière (see above), chilled

Makes 2½ cups

Whip cream until stiff peaks form. Beat chilled Crème Pâtissière until smooth. Using a metal spoon, fold Crème Pâtissière through whipped cream. Refrigerate in an airtight container for up to three days.

Index

little and friday.

Index

Acknowledgements

It was a bumpy time at Little and Friday while writing this book, and I frequently pulled in help from my staff, family and friends to complete it. While I stepped out to write my staff loyally kept the engine going at Little and Friday. I have a great team behind me, with many offering recipes and ideas and also good looks and musical talents as models in various shoots. Thank you to David O'Brien, Kohei Hayashi, Wency Pereira, Freya Adams, Holly Houston and Sophie Beck, for all of your input foodwise in this book.

I was lucky to be paired up with a photographer who is not only brilliant at shooting food but had talent styling, and was so in tune with what I was trying to create. Tam, you made it easy. Thank you so much for going well beyond your role as photographer to make this book what it is.

A very big thank you to our very talented props team: Naomi Bisley, Holly Houston and Estelle Willets for sourcing or making all the props and styling the shoots. Thanks to the boy team who used their muscle to move furniture, props and trays of food up mountains and through rough terrain: Chris Smart, Izaak Houston, Sam Harper and Tom the hammer.

Thanks to Debra Millar and her fantastic team at Penguin Group (NZ) for assisting me when I needed it and for allowing me the freedom of artistic licence, and to Anna Egan-Reid for her fabulous design.

Lastly thanks to all the models, who were either staff or customers roped into our celebrations. Special thanks also to those people who generously provided locations for the photography shoots.

Summer Picnic, pages 11–19
Models: Chris Smart, Blake Rax
Photographed at Mount Victoria, Devonport

Birthday Lunch, pages 20–33
Models: Philippa Bentley, Wendy Smith, Sharon Vallant, Kristin Steel, Bridget Tarr
Thanks to Peter Chichester for the use of his apartment

Kids' Party, pages 34–45
Models: J Steel, Jett Steel, Louis Jourdain, Jonti Dixon, Lily Bisley, Mimi Campbell-Reid, Louis Campbell-Reid

Movie Night, pages 50–65
Models: Lewis Rowe, Selika Shrewsbury, Wency Pereira, Freya Adams
Thanks to the Smith family for the use of their house and garden

Christmas, pages 66–91
Props supplied by Cosi Fan Tutte, Devonport, and Abigails, Devonport; wreath by botanical stylist Annie Oxborough

Wedding, pages 92–115
Models: Tomas and Andreas Marin, Maria Jesusita Barré, Elisabeth Bisley, Hannah Collins, Izaak Houston, Alex Matthews, Sam Harper, Chris Smart
Photographed at Calliope Sea Scout Hall, Devonport; flowers by botanical stylist Annie Oxborough

High Tea, pages 116–129
Models: Eloise Twaddle, Naomi Bisley, Holly Houston, Sol Kim
Photographed at the Wilson Home, Takapuna

Mothers' Day, pages 132–147
Thanks to our good friend Ngaire Saunders

Easter, pages 148–163
Models: Naomi Bisley, Louis Jourdain, Osis Ilohan
Thanks to the Smart family of Devonport

little and friday.